The Secret t
Sober a

A collection of 'Then and Now' tales as sobriety evolves as a positive lifestyle choice.

By Rachel Black

February 2015

Copyright Rachel Black February 2015

No part of this work may be copied or used without prior permission from the author.

This book contains the experiences, thoughts and beliefs of Rachel Black. It is in no way intended as a substitute for professional help. It does not endorse or recommend any one particular sober group, step, or method of becoming and remaining sober. Rather, it recognises that different techniques work best for different individuals and that common to all methods is a desire to modify the relationship we each have with alcohol.

Preface

When I stopped drinking alcohol on 28th March 2013 I was stunned by the black and white changes in all aspects of my life. Nothing else had altered. The changes I noted occurred purely because I had removed alcohol from each situation. Only after I was over the initial OMG! of stopping drinking did I truly realise just how ingrained drinking had become in my life. It coloured everything I did. It influenced all my decisions and affected all the outcomes. My life centred around its presence, doing all that was required to accommodate its ever growing presence. When I wrote my first book Sober is the New Black, I used the popular 'Then and Now' format to compare life before and after. I did this because I thought 'Now' represented the current state of affairs without alcohol, the way life now was. I believed that change to be complete and life would remain this way in the future.

I was not prepared for the way 'Now' would continue to evolve as time passed and my life cycled through its predictable annual events. Each time I revisit a place, an experience or even a memory, I find myself comparing how it was 'Then', how it changed to 'Now', and subsequently how it has changed again to the 'Right now'. I'm sure the change has not stopped here for good either.

Stopping drinking has been less like flicking a switch and more like moving a heavy lever; now that it has been released and started to move, the momentum it gains carries it forwards, moving it indefinitely across the scale, far beyond the last point.

I could not allow my amazement at these changes I continue to notice go unmentioned. Not least of all my emotions about drinking have morphed from initially denying the problem existed, to disappointment as I failed to moderate, and anger when I realised I had to give up, through to being relieved I no longer need to drink, being pleased I no longer have to drink, and finally now being proud I no longer want to drink so I present my evolving impressions of all aspects of my sober life to you here.

Introduction..6
Chapter 1 That Which I Used to Think...9
Chapter 2 My Perception of Sober People 18
Chapter 3 Life, Personality and Hobbies 29
Chapter 4 Sugary Substitutions. 36
Chapter 5 Regrets 45
Chapter 6 The Birthday Party Challenge 49
Chapter 7 Playing Up 57
Chapter 8 Dining Out with Kids 61
Chapter 9 A Typical Weekend 68
Chapter 10 Looking Back 77
Chapter 11 The Cinema 84
Chapter 12 Party Season 89
Chapter 13 A Stressful Day 95
Chapter 14 A Glorious Evening 101
Chapter 15 The One Day Event 107
Chapter 16 Regrets 115
Chapter 17 The Last Train Home 117
Chapter 18 Discretion and Trust 125
Chapter 19 Saturday Night Texting 129
Chapter 20 Regrets .. 136
Chapter 21 Christmas ..141
Chapter 22 Family Commitments .. 152
Chapter 23 First day of Holidays 157
Chapter 24 Now 161

Introduction

Imagine you are in a prison cell. Dark, grey, sad and alone. Now imagine the door is unlocked. You can leave if you want to. You have heard tales of a bright colourful land of opportunity right outside but it sounds too good to be true. Or perhaps it sounds terrifying and you fear leaving your safe surroundings. What if all that's promised doesn't materialise for you?

Worry not. There is a money back guarantee. After leaving through the door, it will remain unlocked. You can return at the cell at any time. If you don't like your new sober life and preferred your old ways, the door will always remain open. Your cell will always be there for you and you can return to it at any point. What have you got to lose?

Once out of your cell you see the path that your new life follows. But the path is not straight forward. At first here are falling rocks to avoid, screeds of gravel where you may lose your footing, sections where the path is indistinct and the way forward is not clear. It is raining and you are cold and the path is convoluted full of twists and turns such you wonder if you are moving forwards at all.

If you persevere through the early stages of this journey, you will be rewarded. The sun will come out and will form the brightest rainbow before the rain subsides. The path will level. It will become wide and clear and you will become confident at navigating your way forwards at the junctions.

You will begin to notice the scenery, the sounds, the wildlife, and you will become distracted. Your journey and the path you are on will slip from the forefront of your mind as it absorbs these new experiences. You meet others along the way and spend time with them, opening your mind to each new experience. Time slows and your journey is no longer hurried. There is no rush to get to the destination because the journey itself is beautiful and you are enjoying every minute of it.

You look back and can no longer see your cell or the treacherous rocks and gravel you first encountered. You have forgotten how difficult it was to start out and persevere on this journey. As you move on you gain confidence to wander off the main path and investigate lesser trails. You become aware of the inherent dangers, the celebrations, the weddings, birthdays, anniversaries, parties, and plan ahead. You plan a strategy to cope with these events and anything else life throws at you. Should your plan prove inadequate, you have an exit strategy too. You have ways and means to find your way back to the main path, the right track, and will not get lost in the wilderness.

After some time you realise you are reaching the end of the rainbow. It is vast and stretches as far as you can see. Life is great. Your health is fabulous. You are solvent. You are a good friend, partner, parent. You are content. You remember. You achieve. Life could not be better.

You hear a shout and look in its direction. Far off the path you see a lone figure stooped in the doorway of a dark, cold, cell, too scared to come out for fear of what lies beyond the confines of their cell. You know the truth about both worlds, inside and out, and you know there is a choice. You can continue to bask in the warm glow of the sunshine or you can crawl back into the cell from whence you came. Why would you?

Chapter 1 That Which I Used to Think...

This week sees me reach two years free from alcohol. I am proud of myself and thankful I stuck (and continue to stick) with it during the difficult times, to enjoy the overall improvement in my life. An understatement if ever there was one.

It struck me recently how differently I view the things I used to think I enjoyed doing. The way my leisure time has changed. The way my thoughts, feelings, emotions, preferences, likes and dislikes have all changed. I thought I knew myself pretty well but the following list, which is in no way exhaustive, shows the apparent misconceptions I held.

I used to think I enjoyed nights out in the pub or drinking at someone's house. I called it a celebration, catching up, or anything else I could conjure up. It was usually me who arranged these nights, me who was motivated to make sure they took place. Now I realise my motivation was purely to engineer a situation conducive to drinking lots of wine. Now I see only those friends whose company I enjoy and instead of drinking we spend time walking and talking or having a simple supper at one of our homes, where I am very happy not to be drinking alcohol and just love the bonus of driving home. Why did I ever think my car was a nuisance? Those for whom drinking is not a problem do not mind doing alternatives which do not involve alcohol.

I used to think I enjoyed having friends and families come around for dinner at the weekend. I spent the day preparing for their arrival: planning, tidying, anticipating. My OH (other half) always seemed a bit perplexed by my efforts and apparent need to socialise but nonetheless went along with the flow I created. I welcomed the children too, up to a point, endeavouring to get them all playing together or absorbed in a DVD accompanied by a steady supply of sugary sweets, leaving us adults undisturbed to socialise and to drink without interruption.

I was in fact, manufacturing excuses to start drinking earlier in the afternoon and to drink more than we would alone on a normal weekend day. Now I wonder how I could ever have been bothered to cook for so many, so often. I hate cooking! The effort I made was huge and for what? So I could drink more and more under the guise of catching up with friends?

I no longer feel the need to socialise with others in our precious free time. I enjoy our weekends pottering around, relaxing as a family, and at times achieving very little. But so what? That is what weekends and down time are all about really.

I used to think I enjoyed socialising with colleagues too and regularly arranged work nights out. The reality of these nights now, without alcohol, confirms I never really wanted to spend time out of work with colleagues at all. Now I choose to avoid all but the odd retirement party I feel duty bound to attend. Additional work nights out were a way to ensure a night where lots could be drunk in the company of like minded people. If everyone is doing the same thing it normalises that behaviour, which is very reassuring.

I used to think I was the heart and soul of the party. Now I realise I was drunk and that 'moving on' to a late night place was merely to keep drinking longer into the night. Now I know the night is over at 11.30pm and am happy to drive home then, if not before.

I used to think I didn't enjoy my home life. It annoyed me. I was dissatisfied by it yet could not see what was missing. Why wasn't it better? I spent a lot of time 'getting away from it all' and 'getting out' for periods of time, leaving OH at home with the kids. Now content, I can see the problem was not the house or my family life or that everything was so difficult. The problem was me. The problem was I needed more and more booze to feel normal. Alcohol only satisfying the need for more alcohol, nothing else, and anything that got in the way of that was a nuisance to be avoided. In recent months I am much more content at home. I am interested. I enjoy jigsaws, have started piano lessons and joined a Spanish class. I can concentrate to read and can watch television without falling asleep. Who knew the pleasures in life could be so simple?

I used to think I enjoyed travelling with work. Meetings and conferences meant a hotel stay, drinks in the bar, a drink in my room as I showered before dinner, pre-dinner drinks, with drinking continuing through the meal and into the small hours of the morning. Conversation centred upon the severity of hangovers, gossip from the night before, and an appraisal of who had been the worst for wear. Working hard and playing hard, living the dream? Now I keep nights away from home to a minimum and go only to events that I cannot avoid, or can travel to and from on a daily basis. I realise these sojourns were a licence for me to drink excessively from the minute I left home. Away from commitments, chores and children, my time was my own to drink, be hungover and subsequently gorge on the rich food provided for us. I no longer arrive home exhausted, worn out and fit for nothing. I am still always glad to come home but now it's for all the right reasons.

One of my main indulgences in life was going out for dinner, particularly as a date type of night with OH. It varied between different restaurants and required little planning or imagination. The conversation would flow: lubricated by alcohol and uninterrupted by children. I really enjoyed these evenings until I stopped drinking. It is so much less appealing now and has become more of a functional outing to eat rather than a proper date which food was only one part of. This is because the bit I enjoyed most about these nights was drinking wine. Starting at home, on an empty stomach (often after a treadmill session) the initial buzz was intoxicating. It continued to be fuelled by more as we chatted and perused the menu and the second bottle slipped down nicely throughout the meal. When OH had dessert, I opted for a large wine by the glass. I liked dessert too but it could not compete with the option of another glass of wine.

I still don't really enjoy going out for dinner much, apart from it being a night off cooking. I really feel the hiatus in that early period and sipping a sparkling water makes me acutely aware that I am not having wine. There seems to be a lot of unnecessary waiting for the food now that a delay is no longer a welcome opportunity to drink more wine and get the second bottle ordered earlier.

I've stopped going out for dinner as often, instead buying quality 'cook at home' food and ask OH to prepare it so I still have a night off from the kitchen.This way I can occupy myself during the preparation stages.

Most evenings I enjoyed a glass of wine. I would usually drink a bottle of wine whilst flicking randomly through magazines, mumbling about how I'd heard it all before, didn't know the current celebs, didn't believe their latest diet claims and many other minute displeasures that annoyed me. When I stopped drinking, I went through a big phase of having ginger beer and savoury snacks in place of wine. I felt the need to substitute wine with another notable drink, keeping some aspects of the habit. Now I have moved to cups of tea and breakfast cereals or biscuits as my habits gradually remodel.

'Before', I would berate myself continually. Too drunk, too hungover, too much food, too much time wasted, feeling awful and so on. Now, I am much kinder to myself. I'm compassionate to myself the way I would be to a friend. If I overeat I acknowledge it, draw the line and move on with the view that I can't change what has happened but I can change how I react to it and what happens next. Similarly if I 'waste' an afternoon, snoozing or doing a jigsaw rather than something more productive, I think this is fine, this is my relaxation time, I can enjoy it. There is no crazy urge to get it all done then flop, officially exhausted, off duty and well deserving of a glass of wine. My life and my mental state are on an even keel nowadays. No crazy extremes from excessive drinking and over compensation.

I used to think I was poor at parenting. Continually irritable and not that interested in child friendly pursuits. Now, I realise I was chronically depressed and hungover. I needed wine, wanted wine and was waiting for the time I could have wine. I am now calmer, more patient, perhaps a little more interested(!) but definitely better rewarded. My children like me more and as they learn about the horrors of addiction at school, they are secure in the knowledge that their mum doesn't drink any wine any more; it almost sounds as if a playground boast!.

I used to wonder what the point to anything was if you weren't drinking alcohol. Now, I think what is the point in drinking? It will be over in a couple of hours and all that will be left is the want for more, followed swiftly by a hangover. The same applies at home. Why drink? It doesn't make the television any more exciting and as our evening time shrinks it's never more than a couple of hours until bedtime. What would I need wine for now?

My book club evenings were another excuse to drink lots of wine. I still enjoy the company of those girls and the chat about the book, and continue to attend. I also notice how no-one drinks as excessively as I thought they did at these nights.Must have just been me.

I no longer have regular cravings but I do, however, miss a glass of wine at times. Or rather, I miss the idea of it, the promise held by that first glass. A night in with friends finds me watching them as their first glass of wine is poured. I think how nice it looks and how I'd love one too. Then I notice perhaps half an hour later that some have barely touched their glass, no one is more than half way through and the pace of consumption is slow. Slower than I would want and I know I would feel unhappy at this stage, my thoughts occupied with ways and means of increasing my supply. My drinking was different. I would drink quickly, offer the top ups, prioritising my own glass, getting another bottle opened, ensuring a third was chilling. This remains very clear to me and I know I never want to go back to being that person. That first cold swirling glass is an illusion. It is not what it seems. To me it represents the unleashing of my own inner demon intent on ruining my evening. So I can resist, I do resist, and I will continue to resist.

Chapter 2 My Perception of Sober People

Then

Way back then I gave very little thought to sober people. They were not on my radar, in fact they were so incomprehensible to me that they may have been from a different planet.

As I got older I started to notice them a bit more and learned about their reasons for being tee-total. One girl in my social circle when I was in my mid twenties had irritable bowel syndrome which was exacerbated if she drank more than half a pint of lager. So that's what she drank each time we were out, and that was all she drank. Nothing more, ever. I felt pity for her and, if I'm honest, mentally discounted her as being any fun. Since then I've had friends with liver problems, unrelated to alcohol, and others with alcoholic relatives who decide not to drink for the sake of their health, they don't want to take the risk or have seen enough to put them off alcohol for life. Whatever the reason, in that period of early adulthood I felt grateful that I was not burdened by any such considerations and could drink whenever I wanted, however much I wanted. And that's exactly what I did.

Somehow I still managed to progress in my career, manage my life and factor in time for my hangovers. Perhaps because it was so much easier being a single girl with no responsibilities to anyone but myself.

As my life passed and I grew up, my social life progressed from a crowd of us standing in a pub drinking beer to one of apparently sophisticated couples at dinner parties awash with wine. I managed to get the vile, bitter taste of wine (yes, really, I remember at first not liking the taste of wine at all-so adept was I at adding a large splash of lime to my pint of lager to sweeten it!). Needless to say, I persevered until I was a fully fledged member of the white or red brigade whose opinions on wine related more to the relative cost of a bottle than any knowledge of, nor interest in its finer points. More was spent on a bottle if visiting; it had to look good enough in case the host waved it around for all to see, or indeed open it that night. It was also justifiable to spend more on a bottle for the weekend as opposed to midweek.

You will have guessed by now that those dinner parties were less about culinary delights, (although some friends did make significant attempts at these) and more about getting drunk with the added bonus of being in safe, like minded company, being able to sit down, stay past closing time, open more bottles as necessary and, if you were the host, no need for a taxi home. It was all so grown up. This was perhaps my first introduction to being able to drink without a finite end to the evening and the beginning of regular drinking at home.

At these nights I felt sorry for those who didn't drink. What was the point? (The irony that I was completely missing the point was lost on me.) How many diet colas or glasses of sparkling water would you want to drink? You see, 'normal' drinks follow conventional rules and obey the laws of diminishing returns. You may really anticipate and enjoy the first drink, but gain less pleasure from subsequent drinks as many of your initial needs have now been met: you thirst is quenched, you've cooled down, you have relaxed, and very rapidly your want begins to fade away. Drinking soft drinks does not make you want more of them. Further, you never check how much is left or wonder if there will be enough because if it runs out it is no big deal. Its job is done.

Wine, or any type of alcohol, does not follow such rules. After the first drink there is only accelerated anticipation and desire for the next. And the next. And the next again. Rather than satisfy a need it seems to incite further desire, necessitating more and more to be taken. It does not quench thirst: it compounds thirst by virtue of its diuretic action so we often have a glass of water at the same time. The sugar load acts in the same way as having a chocolate biscuit before dinner, it kills your appetite but only temporarily. The sugar spike will stimulate insulin release which sends blood sugars plummeting again and before long you will be looking for, craving even, a snack.

Absolved of the body's usual self-regulation of fluids in and out, there are no cues as to when to stop drinking wine. The driving need is never met and there is no off switch to the mechanism, now thoroughly wound up and perpetuated by each glass. In the same way that the only problem solved by food is that of hunger, the point of drinking, as in taking in fluid, is to maintain hydration first and foremost. (Sure there are unnecessary cups of tea we have to procrastinate or to be sociable but this is a more minor consideration.) Wine is exempt from this rule.

Wine is a drug disguised as a drink. It follows the same rules and agenda of any drug in that the only problems it solves are those caused by the lack of it in the first place! That is the perpetual need for more and the agitated state brought on by withdrawal. Its use ensures further use and its further use ensures these uncomfortable feelings return very quickly to encourage continual ingestion. That is addiction.

Those drinking non alcoholic drinks are satisfied by one or two then round off their meal with a cup of tea or coffee. They are comfortable, sated in all senses and are not aware of the misplaced pity felt for them by those throwing back the wine.

In my own circle I thought it a shame these abstainers were missing out, no matter their reasons for not drinking, but I accepted it was their own business and they were free to do as they pleased day to day.

At bigger events and the wider aspects of life I felt truly horrified at the thought of some not drinking at key events. Why would a bride decide not to drink on her wedding day? Why would a new mother not celebrate the birth of her baby and the end of pregnancy enforced teetotalism with a glass of something fizzy and special? How could any true occasion be celebrated without alcohol to make these good times even better? So secure was my belief in this that when Scottish tennis player Andy Murray made history by spectacularly winning Wimbledon in 2013, I watched him enjoying his unique moment of victory knowing that neither he nor his family drank any alcohol and felt sad for them being unable to celebrate his win 'properly' that evening by getting shit faced, because that's the mandatory way to celebrate most events whether good or bad. I wondered if he would feel sad too, depriving himself of a celebratory drink or two to really hammer home his victory and make the best night of his life even better?

It still surprises me how fixed I was in this belief. How indoctrinated I was about the uplifting ability of alcohol to improve everything. To make bad times bearable and elevate good times to some higher plane of pleasure, a special place closed to non drinkers who remain blissfully unaware of such heightened experiences they were missing.

How the sober population must inwardly laugh, shake their heads and wonder if there is any hope for those of us similarly misguided.

Now

Only now, after two years of sobriety, can I understand why brides' mothers and tennis players would choose not to spoil their moments by having alcohol blur it or prevent memories being made. Why would they need to be transported to a higher, magical plane when they want to remain grounded in their lives, fully present to feel these moments entirely?

I never expected to reach this stage. I thought I would live my life without alcohol, and simply accept the pang of regret when not drinking at each special occasion. That I would be glad to simply get through it, get it over and done with, with minimum fuss. I am grateful for the combination of support I had and continue to have, that kept telling me to believe that one day I would be glad I no longer drank and that life would indeed become better. I'm glad I persevered long enough to find this out for myself.

Regardless of your views on AA, my first glimpse of a meeting was of several members chatting outside the building before the meeting started. They were laughing at something clearly hilarious, all of them looking incredibly happy (without alcohol in their lives!). It occurred to me they couldn't all be wrong and they couldn't all be making up a big fat lie about sobriety being okay, or better than just okay: surely someone would break rank and let the secret out of the bag? No, their happiness had to be true. And now I know it was true.

My opinion towards sober people changed again when I realised my drinking was out of hand. As I tried and failed to moderate it, not yet ready to consider giving up totally, I watched sober people with a new sense of awe and admiration which over powered my lack of comprehension of their habits and choices. Why did they do it? *How* did they do it? And how the hell did they do it without feeling deprived, or that their enjoyment was somehow limited? They changed from being unremarkable people with no tales of notoriety, debauchery or extreme behaviour to people I began to seriously consider and observe, possibly admire and envy too.

They appeared content with their ways. Sampling all the delights of an event but not going to extremes. They enjoyed experiences yet knew when enough was enough. They seemed reasonable and sensible and gradually this option became more attractive to me as my drinking continued and my hangovers grew. I began to see more of the positives they enjoyed: a cup of tea with birthday cake, which usually I would not interrupt my flow of wine to have, personal and accessible transport home at an hour of their choosing, when they decided they had adequately celebrated or socialised. No crazy inclinations to go on somewhere open later, to drink all night with people they only vaguely knew yet with whom they had become close and special friends over the last couple of hours.

I began to feel tired of the way I was compelled to behave at such occasions. Always having to drink to excess (or be left wanting), always having to factor in some recovery time and always wondering if this time, I had gone too far and crossed the line from being funny and outrageous to unpleasant, arrogant, disrespectful or simply labelled drunk.

Sober people were aspirational to me as I gave up alcohol. I was a new member of their club and wanted to get in on the act. I found myself commenting on all the aspects of sober behaviour which they had known for years. It reminded me of getting my first smartphone, about five years after all my friends did and loudly sharing my delight at all the things it could do!

'I love deciding just to download a hit right there and then! And a book! Immediately! It's like magic I can do all these things simply from my phone!' I remember exclaiming to my friend.

'Yes, I love my phone' she replied confirming my life long belief that I truly was someone who followed the crowd some significant distance behind.

And now I am one of the sober gang and I felt established there relatively quickly. I realise how normal it has become for me when others moan they have *had* to drive or seem surprised that I am not drinking.

'What, never?'

'Never at all?'

'Not even one?'

'Oh no way could I ever do that, I'd miss a glass of wine too much.'

I can see their train of thought and remind myself that they probably would miss their one glass of wine. The important word being 'one'. That for me is irrelevant. That club is one I never fitted into and I've accepted it now with grace and maturity, in much the same way as I've accepted my skin does not tan in the sun so I no longer persevere with the sun lounger, instead I've turned to fake tan to improve my look. It only took me until my late thirties to arrive at this point!

Chapter 3 Life, Personality and Hobbies

Looking back a few years, I am now an entirely different person. This is not due to an inherent change in my personality, rather that more of the real me has been revealed. Or more accurately, has been allowed to exist without the cumbersome disguise of mind altering substances because now I am comfortable with and accepting of the person I am, with the personality I have always had. Both the good bits and the not so good. The only difference now is they are unmasked and naked, for all to see unfettered.

Then

I was the ultimate Party Girl. The last girl standing: staying out the latest, drinking the most, always up for any night out with anyone who asked, for any reason, because I was 'such a good laugh' and always 'up for it'. And the person I became when I was out in a group was a good laugh. Before it stopped being funny, I was indiscrete, full of gossip and hearsay, witty at the expense of a number of people, whether present or not. I found traits to poke fun at and knew how to unveil weakness and guarantee a laugh from the crowd. I never knew where the line was drawn and often crossed it in ignorance. It was all delivered in a casual, jovial 'we're good friends really, but...' manner and I got away with this most of the time. Even the times when I wondered the next day if my 'friends' actually liked me, really enjoyed my company or were too polite to tell me I'd over stepped the mark and had caused offence with some throwaway comment I had made.

I thought our home life was boring beyond belief. How could OH be happy and content staying in, watching television, listening to the stereo and playing on his i-pad? He drinks alcohol rarely and I considered the poor man dull for a number of years. I was pleased he was happy staying at home. We agreed we were different and he didn't mind me going out with these friends and those friends, without him. I was even more pleased when he decided to treat himself to SkySports. I felt less guilty. He was content to spend time in our lovely house and watch endless golf on the box. This suited me just fine.

It further enabled my social life without him and it meant the children were well looked after by their sensible father during my night out and the following morning when I was incapacitated.

Looking back I'm not sure I had any true hobbies while I was drinking. I didn't really have any time for them, not to mention the tenacity or concentration to pursue them. My life was full of booze management. There was the exercise beforehand to burn the calories I would later drink, the choosing and buying of clothes and shoes to maintain my party girl image and there was time ring fenced for hangover management. This was a passive event consisting of completely clearing a day in my diary, lying on the sofa watching pre-recorded, repeated episodes of something requiring zero concentration, and punctuating the day with toast, scones, sandwiches, cakes and biscuits. Anything to help me feel better sooner.
With time I learned none of these things worked and too much food made me feel even worse. The only thing that helped a hangover was time. I would lie on the sofa internally moaning and wishing the day be done and dusted, that the next would arrive and that I would feel better by that time. I referred to these days as 'write offs'.

Almost always I did feel better the next day, until the latter stages of my drinking career when the hangovers began to last for two full days, sometimes more.

I usually felt sad and full of woe that my life was so awful. I often voiced that the only thing that gave me pleasure was drinking wine and forgetting about said life. I had such blanket discontent yet could not fathom what was missing or what was wrong, and did not know where to begin trying to correct it. I was at a loss. Truly puzzled. All I could do was keep blotting it out with more wine. The worse it got, the more wine I drank. A vicious, descending spiral of despair if ever there was one.

Now

Since stopping drinking I admit I am not the party animal I once was. I no longer need to party until the small hours, find no need to catch up with so many people in such a full on drunken manner and have allowed some of these people to fade from my life. I feel no pressure to uphold any wild reputation I may have had and have no desire to impress by being the best, the thinnest, the funniest, the one who burns the candle at both ends and continues to manage life in between.

I now fulfil my potential but am just as you find me. I'm not trying to be anything I'm not. Why did I feel the need to be that way for so long?

I always felt I could write a book and it was almost the first thing I did as I stopped drinking. I began to take action on all the things I always said I wanted to do yet claimed to never have the time, always being too busy. This was true. I was too busy. I prioritised drinking wine and recovering from drinking wine such that my time was used up and my motivation to change was low. But now I have spare time! It begins at 6pm when previously it ended as the wine was opened and nothing of any worth would be achieved from them on. Now these long evenings where I am present and capable mean I literally have more hours in the day. Isn't that what we all want?

Now in the evening I can do chores to prevent me feeling behind on them at the weekend. I can shop, surf, read and learn responsibly all evening, going to bed when I am pleasantly tired rather than uncomfortably drooling on the sofa.

I've spent time considering the options and choices for re-decorating rooms (well, I organised for the painter to come). I cook for the sake of cooking, to have nice food rather than an opportunity to spend ages in the kitchen alone, drinking wine. Even quick meals took me longer and longer to prepare as they were drawn out and littered with regular sips and top ups.

I feel I can concentrate and choose the amount of time I spend doing things. No longer is life a race against time to get everything done, decided upon and over with as quickly as possible so that, yep, you guessed it, I could get back to drinking wine.

My life has been turned upon its head. It has gone from being so awful I felt the need to escape from it on a daily basis, to being bright and full of opportunity. I feel lucky and alive. Yet at the same time nothing about my life has changed. It continues year after year on its trajectory. What has changed is me. My personality, my outlook, my priorities. These were all so, so wrong and I thought the solution was to drink wine, then drink more wine, until it finally dawned upon me that wine was the cause of the veil obscuring me from my true life. I'm so pleased I drew this back to reveal all that I was missing, before it was too late.

Chapter 4 Sugary Substitutions.

I am addressing my diet problem from tomorrow.

I am vertically challenged such that half an inch here or there really counts. I have always had to actively manage my weight. I've tried loads of methods of staying a normal-ish size but calorie counting always works for me (along with a TON of running and exercise classes) and is the method I always revert to in times of crisis.

It is more accurately described as calorie balancing rather than mere counting. I was disappointed not to lose weight when I gave up drinking but not particularly surprised. I never lose weight 'by accident' or as a side effect to being ill, stressed or worried. I am never so rushed off my feet to be too busy to eat and I never 'forget' to eat.

No, for me weight loss requires hard graft. It always sounded too good to be true that the cloud of stopping drinking would be lined with a new svelte figure by default. The reality is now I am free from the calorific burden of wine I am struggling to maintain any routine or structure to my eating. I am struggling to minimise the gains resulting from my unleashed desire for all things sweet.

Then

I knew a bottle of wine contained 900 calories. I spent my days eating salad and vegetables or diet soup to allow for the wine that evening. I would exercise to allow some snacks too. However, I could never factor in the amount of calories I consumed when I was hungover. To keep at a steady weight meant I ate low calorie food most of the time, exercised a lot and had my wine. I never had dessert. I never ate chocolate. I never ate fast food. Except when I was hungover, then I ate everything!

When the urge came to eat lots I indulged my love of baking cakes. I used to whip up the regular comforting classics: sponge cakes of all varieties, crumbles, oat biscuits, scones and tray bakes. Full of the toxic combination of fat and sugar now being blamed for the obesity epidemic. Then I would eat them. Usually a couple one day when wine had loosened my grip on calories, more the next day to feed my hangover, before polishing of the remainder on the third day when the rest of my family had lost interest in them. These cakes were irresistible and I never tried to resist.

In general, when I was drinking I had a degree of anxiety about gaining weight. I knew wine was exceedingly calorific (and G & slimline T just did not hit the same spot) so I compensated with fewer and fewer food calories and as much exercise as my nauseating hangover allowed. Before a big night out I would exercise throughout the day and eat as little as possible. If eating out I would choose the salad (dressing on the side), no starter (more wine time whilst stomach empty) and definitely no dessert. Not even a consideration. Never.

And all this micro-management worked to a degree. Largely, my weight stayed acceptable (although I must have been malnourished) despite fluctuating with frequent morning after the night before all you can eat carb and junk food feasts.

Now

When I stopped drinking, I did not lose weight. On the contrary; my anxiety has gone, I am more relaxed about everything and I struggle not to gain weight. Loss of anxiety is usually a good thing but being more relaxed about my eating and weight means 'Yes, I'll just have that, no, it doesn't matter, and of course I'm having dessert'. The excuse of not having wine and therefore having lots of spare calories to use did not cover half of what I would eat.

In the last few months I have tried endless diets, (read 'moderation'). And guess what? It doesn't work. At least not for me. I've tried and failed so often it reminds me exactly of my attempts at moderating wine. I cannot do it.

So I'm trying to tackle my biscuit laden diet the same way. By having none at all. Not even one. Not even for a treat or on a special occasion, in an attempt to break the cycle of failure and to eat clean, eat when I'm hungry and eat nutritious foods rather than simple snacky carbohydrates laden treats. I've heard about the horrid three day cold turkey phase experienced as carbohydrates are lowered and sugar stores eliminated. Headache and lethargy develop, the inactivity compounding the feeling of being perpetually cold. Previously on low or no carb jaunts I've never lasted beyond 36 hours due to these symptoms. But this time I'm determined to roll with it and ride the storm, putting my faith in those who have done it before me, who promise it gets easier with time and tell me I will never look back. Just as those sober for longer than me did the same to encourage me through the difficult start of that journey. I know it won't be easy but then neither was giving up wine. Perhaps I've forgotten how excruciatingly difficult those first three days with no wine actually were?

As I said to myself on the first day of going alcohol free, if I don't make the change now, what will it take to make me do it? How bad does it have to get? How often do I need to repeat the same mistake? And as before, I'll be doing the sugar avoidance one day at a time. Abstaining only for today, never committing further ahead than that. Tomorrow is a whole day away and I will leave making any decisions about it until then.

I am maintaining the same weight-just, but I am struggling to do so. The effort not to gain weight is as great as running as fast as I can yet not moving anywhere. I'm less strict about my calorie intake and I have stopped writing down all that I eat, partly because my anxiety over such things was associated with drinking and has now gone, but partly due to my over-riding attitude of 'previously I would have been having wine so...'

which makes the whole calorie in/out, weight loss/gain equations seem much less important to get right. Maybe getting dressed up and going out less often is a factor too. The pressure to look good no longer a prominent concern of mine. Difficult though my weight management is, I still prefer my new simpler life by far. I'm much more lax, and I allow myself to enjoy many more treats without adhering to a punishing exercise regime in advance.

My lack of exercise is mainly due to lack of prioritisation but honestly, I have never enjoyed exercising. My aim was always more about the calorie burn and what I could then eat while still balancing the calorie books, than about any great desire to get fit. I've decided I'm not doing it anymore. I'm not going to spend time making myself do something I hate and I'm not going to dwell on the fact that I ought to be doing it and and am not. I'm having a total break. Life's too short.

However, my weight and eating patterns are now beginning to get me down. I am overeating more frequently and cannot deny the weight creep any longer. Unless I stop it and reverse the trend my clothes will 'shrink' and I will become depressed about it. I've toyed with removing refined sugar (you know, the white addictive one) from my diet for several months but I eat so many biscuits throughout each day that even the thought of a change of this magnitude terrifies me into procrastination and delay in actually doing anything.

Until now that is. The latest book I read on this subject was such simple stuff, blunt and straight talking, a bit like Jason Vale but for sugar! Basically, it said if you keep doing what you're doing, you will keep getting what you're getting. It's not rocket science but just seeing it written down drives it home more effectively. As with many similar motivational phrases, 'Stop Thinking. Start Doing!' it is easy to keep talking the talk and so much harder at the first crunch point when you begin to walk the walk too. And just as I was with wine, I am sick and tired of making the same mistakes over and over again and wondering why I never succeed, why the outcome is never any different. A lot of the soundbites remind me of giving up wine: 'Don't take the first bite', 'This craving too, will pass', 'What pleasure does it really bring you?'.

I've tried to bend the rules as far as they will go. I made banana and blueberry muffins with multiple substitutions to reduce the sugar spike and subsequent trough cycle. I shopped especially for rapeseed oil (in place of butter) and Cow and Gate apple puree pockets (instead of sugar filled adult variety to accompany lamb, which is a fraction of the price!). I used wholemeal flour. I didn't have honey so I added extra yoghurt and a little stevia (the natural calorie free sweetener). I was unsure if the resulting consistency was correct. I know it's not clever to play around with recipes in this random manner, particularly when one has no innate baking skills but I was intent on making a cake that I could eat while maintaining my sugar free plan. All 12 muffins came out of the oven in their pretty little cases and looked beautiful. I photographed them displayed on my pretty tiered cake stand, all looking lovely.

But they tasted awful.

They tasted of nothing really, and were just pieces of non-descript, bland, cake-like texture. My camera was lying and I reflected that it was a bit like drinking non alcoholic wine: it is just not the same without certain key ingredients such that you have to question the point of it.

To give up sugar a total change was required and I was still searching for a way that would click with me. Learning from techniques I learned about alcohol and drinking I decided to stop trying to give up sugar. Instead I would choose to set myself free from its destructive clutches, one day at a time.

This remains a work in progress. I have fallen off the wagon many times and have not yet reached the stage of accepting that sugar laden food is not what I actually want. I keep trying. Only by giving up can you fail to achieve a goal. Each time you get back up another battle begins and eventually, at some vague point in the future, the war will be won.

Chapter 5 Regrets

My regrets from my drinking days are not the times when I was most drunk, most sick, most sleepy, most embarrassed, or mortified. Rather, my regrets are times I look back upon and feel bad and sad about the way they were negatively affected by alcohol.

Like many, I had great plans for my 40th birthday. It was an age and stage I wanted to mark for all the right reasons. My head was no longer in the sand about my drinking and I was beginning to realise, though not necessarily accept, that I could not moderate my intake and would have to stop for good sometime, soon perhaps, but never right now.

I made my first serious attempt to give up booze about six months before my birthday. I went to AA. I read the literature. I met members for coffee. I went the whole hog. I looked ahead to the glittering party I was planning, thinking of how I would invite all my new sober friends. They would know of my struggle and would be delighted to have me join their ranks. It would be as if I belonged to a secret club. I envisaged basking in self satisfaction as I toasted my achievement with sparkling water.

Alas, my attempt was not successful. Like any new fad (to me) I went all guns blazing for the first two weeks and then floundered when the novelty wore off. It became too hard. What was the point? It was my 40th birthday for goodness sake! I was hardly going to drink all my life and then stop just before one of its biggest celebrations to date, was I? That would be daft. No, why not just put the sobriety thing to one side for now and revisit it at some vague point in the future? Perfect.

The day of my party arrived.

I feel I ought to say I enjoyed it. On many levels it delivered much of what I had wanted. A smart venue, a good crowd, nice food and plenty of booze flowing. It was spoilt only by me getting too drunk.

I had started the evening with a strict plan. I would have one glass of bubbly as I greeted guests on their arrival. I would drink wine only with food, at the table. I would spend the majority of the night on the dance floor, pleasantly drunk but not overly so, and quench my thirst with diet coke, having only enough alcohol to keep me nicely topped up. If anyone asked to buy me a proper drink I would choose gin and tonic, which at the time I could drink endlessly it seemed, without becoming inebriated the way I did with wine.

The plan went out of the window early on. I stood at the entrance, next to a tray of pink fizz and handed them out on a 'one to you, one to me' basis as the guests arrived.

I had a large glass of white wine with my meal and then toured the tables talking to everyone. I had a new glass of wine at every table. I recall thinking of how I had planned to stop drinking wine when the meal ended but a finite definition of that time hadn't been made and never materialised. The evening merged on to the cake (and coffee) stage followed by the disco.

It's always the case that drunk people want others to join them and I was no exception. I became quickly disappointed as my like-minded friends cried off from excessive partying one by one. There was an upset stomach, an upset child, an upset babysitter, a car to be driven, an early start the next day and a hangover from the day before. All of a sudden it seemed as if everyone was on their best behaviour except me.

I was annoyed by this and personally offended too. I felt it said my party was not good enough to merit getting plastered at and no-one had bothered to push the boat out for this occasion of mine. I wanted my gang to get drunk with me and for us all to have a ball together.

The consequence was that I spent a lot of time dancing alone, all alone, on an otherwise empty dance floor. My inhibitions were long gone and I had reached the stage of inebriety required to believe I was on a par with Kylie or Beyonce. A couple of friends joined me for brief episodes when our favourite tunes were played; I suspect they felt embarrassed for me and only did it out of pity. Whatever the reasons, their hearts were not truly in it the way I had envisaged.

All in all it was a big disappointment and sadly not one of my best party nights despite all my planning and organisation. Part of me was sad as I remembered my vague plan to celebrate my 40th sober, truly signalling that a new stage of my life was beginning. Alas it wasn't to be and I turned 40 in much the same manner I had marked every occasion for the last 20 years.

Chapter 6 The Birthday Party Challenge

I hosted a birthday party for my daughter and several of her nine year old friends. Now it's over and I'm sitting with a large mug of tea and quite possibly an even larger piece of birthday cake, I can't help but reflect on the differences between today and her parties of previous years.

Then

In the initial baby years, before children know it's their birthday, we invited similar families around to our home. I put on a buffet and they brought a present for the baby. I was extremely anxious about it. I felt a homemade cake was expected, I wondered if the food was good enough, and whether there was enough of it.

We all had a glass or two (or three) of something fizzy to mark the baby turning one or two. The party and the drinking started in the afternoon as guests came and went, but for me the drinking continued long after the last guest had left. There would be an unwelcome interruption when the birthday baby wouldn't settle immediately at 7pm, after a quick dunk in the bath and a rush through the bedtime routine, before my drinking could continue until my own bed time.

But, we had young children! Not only did we deserve to kick back and relax, we actually *needed* to do so in order to cope. Collapsing into a large glass of wine was the well accepted way to achieve this. Drinking wine was confirmed mummy folklore, openly talked about on Mumsnet along with cute references such as wine time, wine o'clock and mummy's special juice. My circle of friends were all doing exactly the same, or so I assumed from their conversations. Whether they were doing it to the same extent as me is unclear, but we all certainly talked in similar terms. No one questioned the wisdom of it. It was just what we did and that made it normal.

We progressed to years of hosting childrens' parties at soft play centres. I was less stressed by these but hated the noise. To this day I cannot bear those places. They promise the perfect afternoon: your children play, you sit in an oasis of calm with a coffee and a slice of home made cake, reading one of the thoughtfully provided celebrity magazines.

They never deliver this ideal..

I found myself spending the time getting up and down continually. Rescuing them from the top of a slide, finding socks, taking them to the loo or yelling at them to stop fighting. But the worst thing is still the noise level.

During a child's party, the noise level is amplified, and I coped by watching the clock as I endured it, looking ahead to the time when the shoes were put back on and the party bags given out. When it was all done and dusted I could head home reassured I had done the good mother bit and was now understandably exhausted.

When the time arrived I was impatient to be gone, desperate to collapse with my glass of wine and put up my own official 'Closed' sign, no longer interested in the event or available for any other sort of requests for attention. My focus was getting back to business as usual, drinking wine on the sofa, 'relaxing,' and having no one ask anything of me.

I once felt sorry for the children at these parties. I wondered how they could possibly enjoy themselves without the promise of alcohol hanging in the air. I thought how let down they must feel when it was over, going home without the option to drink! I honestly thought their little lives were lacking in something that wine could provide.

Now we have progressed on to home based craft parties involving smaller numbers of children of an age where they no longer cry to express their every want and need.

Three years ago on this day, I was at day 19 of one of my previous unsuccessful attempts at giving up alcohol. I felt agitated and anxious before the party, about nothing in particular, just everything in general. I rushed around tidying the house to within an inch of its life and fidgeted with napkins until they were just so.

I remained anxious during the party. I herded the guests around the programme of spongy sticker mosaics, happy birthday cake time, pin the tail on the donkey and finally provided a party tea of pizza. By the time the children were collected I was frazzled, completely strung out and I felt as if I would never relax in a million years.

There was no time to do so either. We were leaving immediately to meet the grandparents for another birthday celebration, this time in a child friendly restaurant.

My current moderating regime was to allow myself to drink alcohol once per month and I had identified this month's drinking night would be the following week when I was due to travel and be away overnight with work. So near, yet so far.

I needed to drink now though. What difference would a few days make? I was almost there anyway, and besides, this was no whim for a glass of wine. No, this evening I knew I truly *needed* wine, while simultaneously hating the fact that it was, indeed, a need.

I decided I was going to drink at the restaurant.

I drank two large 250ml glasses of wine swiftly before I began to relax, my tension giving way to my incessant, opinionated monologues. I tried not to think too much about breaking my own rules. Objectively it was only one more night in an otherwise sober month, bringing the total number of drinking nights that January to two.

But it wasn't just one more night.

After deviating from the plan, the new trajectory continued and I drank the following night too. And the next, and the next again, for almost a week until my planned trip away came up. There seemed no point in trying to stop for the brief interim period of a couple of days when another event was planned so soon; one at which there was no option but to drink, as I truly believed.

The feeling that I had failed again and could not do this giving up booze thing was overwhelming and I felt down. There was no pleasure in being released and allowed to drink again. Only feelings of despair and bewilderment and thoughts such as 'here we go again'. How could I not manage to do that which I professed to want so much?

The reality was that I *could* give up. Of course I could. There was only me pouring the drinks and lifting the glass to my lips. No one was forcing me or even encouraging me to drink The problem was deeper, almost subconscious. I didn't want to give up. I wanted to moderate but seemed reluctant to accept that I was unable to do so.

Now

I made the birthday cake the night before the party. It looked nice, undoubtedly wonky enough to confirm it was indeed homemade! I coaxed the girls through the stuffing and stitching of cuddly pandas, puppies and penguins and completion of birth certificates for said animals.

Next they made bookmarks and later I presided over the chocolate bar game and provided a birthday tea of sausage rolls and chips, all the while wondering what had been so difficult about it the last time? What had made it so stressful that I needed wine afterwards?

I chatted to my daughter's friends and felt like the birthday party *was* the event rather than something to be endured, until the real business of drinking could begin, the reward for my efforts.

This year I enjoyed the party rather than wishing it be over. Honestly I did. I felt exhausted afterwards but tidied up, mopped the floor then flopped in the quiet of the lounge with a cool glass of sparkling water. OH popped his head in to ask whether he should cook dinner for us that evening? (A needless question really but I truly appreciate this offer anytime it is made.)

He did cook and it was a simple but delicious meal which left me feeling full, relaxed and happy.

I'm not sure if I'm more happy about not spoiling my evening by drinking or knowing that I won't be hungover tomorrow. The underlying fact is the same: I am happy *not* to be drinking and this proves yet another aspect of my life has turned out to be better without alcohol despite my skepticism.

The case against booze stood strong at the Birthday Party test.

Chapter 7 Playing Up

Then

My resolve to abstain was tested to the limit one day on holiday when my children, then aged nine and seven, were driving me mad, had been doing so all day and 4pm arriving on a day like today was a huge trigger to dissociate from them and concentrate on drinking.

By 5pm OH was having a rare beer. I really felt like having not a glass, but a bottle of wine to numb my anger at the kids and to forget about them for a few hours. To feel dreamy and be selfish for an hour or so. Despite the knowledge that this was akin to stepping off the merry-go-round for a brief period before jumping back on as it whizzed around at speed, I still wanted to drink. Badly.

I was almost one year alcohol free and this was the second holiday I had dealt with in that time, as well as many other challenges. I had reached the stage of trusting myself pretty much all the time and as much as my want to escape was that night, I just knew I wouldn't actually drink. The stubborn person inside me refused to be beaten, refused to spoil my impeccable AF achievement over a couple of moaning kids. I don't know where the strength or courage came from at that moment but it definitely reared up when most needed.

Instead I voiced my conflicted feelings to OH and in return received some consolatory words confirming how difficult the children could be.

I filled the empty space inside me with a pizza instead of the salad I had planned to have for dinner, and followed it with a large ice cream. Different ways to quell the angst inside of me. Next, I brought the day to a premature end by packing the kids off to bed early and doing the same myself.

We watched a movie in bed and I enjoyed this. It took the focus of my attention away from my internal turmoil. It served to give me the child free space and time I needed, that my head needed and which was no longer forthcoming from a bottle of wine. I was aware the film was helping the time to slip by and that the next day would come in due course. It would be a different day, hopefully a much better one.

And it was. In the morning I was glad not to be hungover, still seething at the kids and now angry at letting myself down too. I was glad yesterday had passed and I had survived relatively unscathed. I had changed my usual reaction to a given situation and that made me feel powerful, invincible, and in control. Buoyed by this success I felt if I could do that, I could do anything now.

It wasn't easy but sustaining long term goals does become more difficult at times. I am learning from each experience and arming myself with a variety of weapons to use the next time I reach a crossroads on the sober path.

Now

At two years sober there are still challenging times and there is still a need to disappear and a want to blot them out. What has changed is the range of options I now have to achieve that state of detachment from an acute stressor.

Recently, I received two separate pieces of shocking family news during a telephone call. They left me displaced, far from my comfort zone both physically and emotionally. I cried and cried and cried, hiccoughing, sobbing, coughing, blowing my nose and trying to talk through my tears as I questioned everything. I needed to escape more than ever. It was too much all at once, far exceeding my capacity to deal with it.

Only a short while later I had exhausted myself of tears and was now wailing, hollow howls of hurt with the purpose of letting at least something out.

When that drew to a close I lay down on the sofa with my head on OH's knee; thoroughly spent and devoid of rational thought. I promptly fell asleep and remained dead to the world until awoken at midnight by OH telling me it was time to move upstairs to bed.

I went through the motions of brushing my teeth and getting changed like a zombie. On some level though, I acknowledged the evening had passed and I was safe.

My coping strategies remain fairly constant. An absorbing movie or something to eat, inducing exhaustion either with strenuous exercise (swimming is good if you can get yourself there at the time) or total mind and brain wipe-out (not recommended), or you can simply sit with the discomfort, acknowledging the unpleasant feelings and waiting for them to pass.

They will pass. They always do. It is hard, but nothing worthwhile is easy.

Chapter 8 Dining Out with Kids

Having dinner in a restaurant with the kids represented a huge change from doing so as a couple, yet I endeavoured to keep up the tradition of a meal out equalling lots of wine, despite the odds being stacked against this.

Then
The point of the evening was to avoid cooking, planning, and preparing a dinner only to have someone scream that they do not like what you have made. And, as ever for me, going out meant drinking wine. Previously, before having kids, dining out was an evening of romance or extreme drunkenness parading as 'letting our hair down'. It becomes difficult to hang onto these traditions with small children, but despite this, I gave it a good try for several years.

Firstly I ensured I was not the driver. Luckily OH usually volunteers for this role or does not mind if I volunteer him for the job. He likes driving more than drinking.

Next was to try and enjoy a drink before we went out. This could go one of two ways: either it was a success and allowed time for me to have 'enough' and begin to relax, or it could induce the first of many interruptions to my drinking world, setting the format for a fraught evening ahead.

At the restaurant we would immediately be presented with the full menu and asked what we would like to drink. There is a definite keep-it-moving feel when dining out with children, even in the most family friendly of restaurants. There is a general rushed approach to everything borne of the need to prevent children becoming over hungry or bored.

I have to think quickly because asking for the wine menu means at best a delay in actually receiving the drink or at worst, being totally forgotten about. Not yet seated, I quickly order a glass of anything white by the glass.

'What size would you like?' he asks.

I pause, as if to consider my answer before nodding and stating 'I think I'll have the large tonight' in a just-for-a-change, now-you-mention-it, why-the-hell-not' manner. I'm sure it fools no-one (except perhaps myself). A large glass is necessary because you never know when the opportunity to order another will present itself, and if by chance it is sooner rather than later, you can always drink more quickly!

With drinks ordered, food decisions have to be made. Kids need to be starving to eat what's put down to them so reading the menu cannot be the prolonged episode preferred by drinkers characterised with smiling apologies: 'Can you give us another five minutes please?' followed by 'Sorry we've been talking and not had a chance to look yet! Yes, another glass would be great thanks'.

No. With children present food is ordered swiftly.

Not only that but it tends to arrive quickly too. Any interim pause is likely to be filled with tears over unequal distribution of the breadsticks or a broken crayon in the colouring kit. That is if you are lucky enough to avoid a drink being knocked over and the ensuing razzmatazz of napkins and raised voices. The result is there is little or no time to drink between ordering and eating.

As any parent will tell you, if you want your food hot, you eat it as soon as it is served and as quickly as possible whilst being required to open ketchup, cut up potatoes and wipe faces. I did not enjoy drinking wine while I was eating and particularly not when eating in a hurry. It seemed wasteful somehow, using wine to quench thirst (apparently) between mouthfuls rather than sipping it unadulterated. But quaff it I did, beggars can't be choosers after all.

Dessert time for everyone else provided a decent window of time for another glass of wine for me. It too would be sub-optimal as I would be full from having eaten and with my restraint removed by the two preceding glasses, I sampled 'just a mouthful to try it' of everyone else's dessert.

I would leave the restaurant thoroughly dissatisfied by the quality and quantity of wine I had been able to drink. I was driven home and would continue the search for nirvana, setting the scene to really enjoy the next glass of wine

This rarely happened either as by this time I was drunk enough to have gone off the taste of it yet had missed out on the transient high of early inebriation. Drinking now only compounded the negative. But that was no reason to stop when the night was still young.

Why did I ever think everything was better with a bit of wine thrown in when it appears to be the cause of great disappointment, despair and dissatisfaction in the episode above?

Now

Dinner with kids is a functional event where the aim is to get everyone fed without any preparation or washing up. It is not a time to linger and it is not particularly relaxing. Once I accepted this and went with the flow, it became much more enjoyable than battling against the tide, trying to fit the wine drinking of before within the constraints that come with children. Keeping expectations low increases satisfaction no end.

Dinner can be a time for conversation, sometimes involving all of us and may even allow spontaneous comments about life at school, to be aired and shared. Since the invention of i-pods and our relenting to allow their use at the table, it has become just the two of us thinking of things to say to each other, more often than not.

Time to peruse the menu is limited after ascertaining the childrens' final choices in view of their rapidly changing minds. Against a background of mild anxiety ensuring drinks are not spilt, it's pretty plain sailing. I don't mind the inconvenient requests for toilet visits nor the classic times at which they occur (at least this usually guarantees the food will arrive!). I am pleased to no longer be annoyed at this intrusion which once disrupted my flow of wine. I'm proud of being a totally sober parent unlikely to fly off the handle or bark threats because I'm only half way drunk and being prevented from getting completely so.

It's fun too. Taking photos of our food, choosing our desserts, discussing who should pay and, our favourite, people watching. My children have inherited my pass remarkable nature and together we laugh at 'crazy shoes' or outfits we deem 'not a good look'. I surprise myself when I laugh, properly out loud, at our observations, without even a drop of booze.

But at the same time I feel smug. I want to call out 'Look at me! I don't need to drink to have fun, I don't need to drink to get through dinner as this restaurant visit is no longer such an ordeal'. I don't say these things aloud but I look around and notice who drinks what, how many they have, how they look, and how they catch the waiter's eye to order the next. I notice all these things because I know the signs of someone who is dependent, someone needing more than the situation allows, and although I feel sober and superior, I retain great empathy for these people. I know how bad it is. I know they can't see any other way and at times I have to stop myself approaching them, telling them what I observe and asking them to believe me when I say that a different way of life is possible and can be enjoyable.

I will never actually do this because I've learned that you can only stop drinking when you are at your wits end, so fed up with your lot that you *want* to give up booze no matter what price you must pay. When that time comes, those who are brave enough take the first step and stick with the promise and belief that while it is hard at first, it will get easier with time and experience.

Chapter 9 A Typical Weekend

Had you asked me two years ago how I spent a typical weekend, I would have told you I am always out on a Friday night, prefer to stay in on a Saturday night and have friends around on Sunday. This weekend routine was almost entirely centred around booze.

Then

Friday night. I love it. It's my favourite night of the week, the start of the weekend which stretches out ahead, full of free time, opportunities and indulgence. Hopefully, I'm not too hungover from celebrating the end of my working week on Thursday night (when an additional glass of wine is allowed before my day off on Friday), and will be well enough for my planned night out.

Latterly I had manufactured a very busy social life and went out with one of various groups of friends each and every Friday night, no exceptions. If there was nothing planned, I planned it. Even if it meant inviting the girls round to mine, there would be a boozy night of some sort guaranteed.

Then on the Saturday I hoped to be functional enough to get up in time for the 9am exercise class at the gym and go to it despite a fuzzy head and groggy lethargy.

Later, I tried to look after the kids without too much distemper. (I was going to say I tried my best but in all honesty it was never my best effort, it was whatever I had left to give whilst preoccupied with my hangover.)

I would struggle to get through the afternoon without a binge on biscuits or cake, even when I knew they would stretch and distend my stomach uncomfortably and would subsequently prevent the high from wine being taken on an empty stomach.

In the evening, I would cook a nice meal for me and OH. My definition of a 'nice meal ' was one accompanied with and defined by a free flow of wine. No waiting on waiters to open it or queueing at the bar. Cooking, even partly prepared oven ready food, provided an excellent opportunity to start drinking earlier. A starter prolonged the drinking time available before the main meal and dessert would be for OH only. I didn't do desserts; did not enjoy mixing them with wine so would feel 'entitled' to an additional large glass of wine instead.

With no transport issues or babysitter to consider, the drinking continued unabated until bedtime. OH would have had one glass of wine lasting from before the starter, well into the main course. He may have a top up during dinner but that would be it for him. I would have the rest and there was always plenty more in the fridge. I was orchestrating the evening and had sole charge of the purchasing and supply of wine. I could drink as much as I wanted without comment. OH never commented negatively about my drinking. I'm sure he must have noticed (although he does often miss significant details). He was either too diplomatic to say anything or did not think it was problematic. Possibly the latter and then probably because he only saw half of it.

On these nights the conversations were in-depth, animated, and enjoyable until I became increasingly drunk, irrational and overly emotional about something or other. This resulted either in us having an argument or me over-reacting and being in floods of tears.

I felt these nights were somewhat spoilt if the kids did not stay in their beds and interrupted my exclusive wine time. I did not see it was my reaction to their needs that spoilt the evening: seething with resentment and irritation.

On Sundays I woke up and assessed my degree of symptoms before lifting my head. I was pleased if I wasn't too nauseous (some nausea was inevitable if I had more than one bottle of wine). I would have juice and paracetamol first and with OH out at golf I would spend the morning eating cereal and toast, feeling more and more awful as time went on.

Managing our household food and drink to accommodate these events and ensuring there was no chance of the wine running out meant I had no time to keep up with the housework or to do the ironing. I was forever running to the shops and when I did have free time I usually needed a sit down to recover from the night before. I am fortunate that I could pay a cleaning lady to come in, and I sent the ironing out. Life was such a whirlwind: here I was 'having it all', it's no wonder I needed some help with the mundane chores of running a home.

I thought our family life was dull and boring so usually invited a similar family around 'for family dinner' on Sundays. This was an earlier dinner, mindful as we were of the following 'school day'. Their kids were invited too and this kept our own two happy and in need of less adult attention.

The routine was that the ladies started the first bottle (often something pink and fizzy) on arrival at 3pm. We would feed the kids at 4pm, opening the second bottle in advance of 5pm when the adult dinner was planned.

I would keep drinking all evening. (I assumed my friends did too when they returned home but now I suspect that leaving my house marked their evening being over).

At the kids bedtime, I left OH to shepherd them through their bathroom routine and into bed while I busied myself in the kitchen, drinking more wine, nibbling left over snacks and slowly tidying away.

When all was done and the kids were settled I would finally relax in the quiet of the lounge with a crisp cool glass of wine. I was exhausted. Tomorrow, Monday, would bring the start of a two day hangover and three days of gloom, perpetuating my thoughts that life was boring, depressing, totally rubbish. Thank goodness I had wine to perk it up. Wine was my saviour. How would I survive without it?

Now

I still love Friday nights; they mark the beginning of my weekend. I can drive home on a wet, dark Thursday night and look forward to my day off with optimism. Paradoxically, given Friday is my day off, I spring out of bed more easily, eager to get on with the day.

I still spend the evening having 'me' time. In between taxi runs to and from various kids' clubs I have a 90 minute interval which I spend as my mood dictates. Whether in a local cafe reading a book or staring into space, browsing around the shopping centre or swimming (relaxing in the sauna and steam room more accurately), I have some lovely quiet time which I enjoy. I truly feel I am the luckiest person alive and do indeed have it all when I have an enjoyable evening out or in, followed by feeling just as good, if not better the next day.

On Saturdays I fill the mornings with hairdresser appointments, shopping for errands, more pleasurable retail therapy, and I try to meet at least one friend for a good 60 minutes of walking and talking in the park (we call it our mutual therapy).

I buy special food for the weekend, choosing foods I know we each enjoy and spending money on items I once thought extortionate while simultaneously not turning a hair when paying over the odds for several bottles of wine (always by card so I didn't feel as if I was parting with so much money). Somehow buying more expensive wine makes the drinking of it more legitimate, in my mind anyway.

Our Saturdays are full, taking the children to and from their various activities. I have little time for myself and now wonder how I had time to be hungover? I take pride in my home and enjoy tidying it up, feeling a sense of personal satisfaction when it is all in order. I still have cleaning help, mainly because I like the house to be more clean than my natural inclinations would achieve! I enjoy ironing: I bought a super duper steam iron as a treat to myself to whizz through the shirts and uniforms (living the dream, I know). It makes me feel as if I am looking after my family properly when I see hangers full of clean laundry waiting to be put away. I *can* cope and feel content now, rather than being over whelmed and eternally behind with chores I was not capable of doing. It's the simple things sometimes I guess.

Saturday night entertainment is variable. We had a phase of family movie which involved meeting on the sofa at 7.30pm having had a bath and changed into pyjamas (sometimes not only the children). We have had routine cinema trips and more special evenings at the theatre, broadening our horizons with some niche performances. Other times we are content to stay in, leave the television off and chat, read or do our own quiet thing. It sounds so dull but I love the calm stability of it all, using the weekends to relax and recuperate just as they were designed for.

Sundays are for leisure. I no longer have any inclination to have a houseful of guests each afternoon and cannot help but think how I must have put the needs of my own family second to my desire to orchestrate a party.

After his golf, I have the afternoon to do with as I choose. I meet friends, walk, go swimming or shopping, either alone or with my daughter. Increasingly, as she gets older, our time together is truly enjoyable and I am introducing her to my shopping habits; the tiring business of trying on clothes and the recuperative visit to a coffee shop. Spending time with her in this way gives me an internal warmth and glow. I'm relieved I am able to do this and bond with her before her teenage years. I'm relieved it is pleasant for both of us and not spoiled by me being of low mood and easily aggravated.

We still have family dinner, but now it's only the four of us and we eat together. We sit at a set table in the dining room and all eat the same meal. I like to think my children have learnt table manners and have the propensity to like or at least try, most vegetables. This has been helped in part by focussing on eating together as opposed to me drinking apart from them.

I feel bad in lots of ways as I write down the way I spent my time before, how although I was present, I was not fully there for my children when they were younger. However, I also know there is nothing I can do to change that. The past is passed. Instead I try to quash my guilt by being grateful that I stopped drinking when I did and managed to change my ways before my children grew up and began to notice how much their mother drank.

Chapter 10 Looking Back

As I start my third year alcohol free I thought I would look back, to reflect upon and share with you, the changes in my thoughts, feelings and actions as my sober time has accumulated. The diary I kept in my first few weeks of giving up alcohol shows the aspects of life in which the most remarkable changes have taken place.

Mood and motivation.
This is a big one for me and it definitely improved early on. When I would let myself think about wine, I wondered how I would cope if, or perhaps when, I was next tempted. I wondered if, by spending so much time reading sober blogs, sober books and chatting on sober networking sites, it was becoming all too consuming? Was I making mountains out of molehills? I decided I was not. I needed to read the almost daily accounts of others who had been alcohol free for so long before feeling confident enough

to try drinking again. They would plan, and try to moderate, thinking they would be able to do so this time, before reporting that they were back to square one in no time at all. Without exception, each regretted the backward step, and urged others not to try it.

No-one blogs that they have inexplicably become able to moderate and are glad they returned to drinking, doing so sensibly this time. It just does not happen. Such accounts provided timely reminders that this too, would be my fate if I became lax or blase about alcohol.

Around seven weeks alcohol free I had been feeling really down and a bit disillusioned about what sobriety had to offer. Reading these tales reinforced the fact that wine will not change this feeling. It may blot it out for a brief period, but will not, ever, improve it.

Since stopping only a few weeks before, I had not 'written off' a day through being fit for nothing and have been grateful every morning I awoke without a hangover.

Today I am still grateful for that each morning. My hangovers were terrible; all encompassing and completely prohibitive.

My Drinking Head.

This is definitely much quieter now. I do not think about alcohol routinely. The 'will I, would I, could I, should I' internal debate has vanished but I cannot pin point when exactly this happened. Thoughts of drinking are off my radar now, for the vast proportion of time.

At weekends my thoughts are more 'What will I have or do that will be enjoyable and fun, kind and nurturing? How will I treat myself?'.

If I'm going out my default position is now to drive. With time I feel less and less as if I may be missing out on something when not drinking in a restaurant. It seems the bubbly period of feeling merry is over very quickly, almost as soon as the food arrives.

I think the peak period of enjoyment during drinking episodes happens quite early on. I watch others continuing to drink past this point, oblivious to it, seeking the ultimate climax. Perhaps they are unable to stop. Or perhaps they just don't realise the peak has passed and time is up. By continuing to drink at this point they merely postpone the time their inevitable hangover will kick in. When they do finally realise the night is over, it is too late to avert the disaster and impending doom.

The delight that I've had an enjoyable evening with absolutely no price to pay the next day fills me with the kind of child-like glee seen only on Christmas morning.

I know my change to AF is a permanent one: it was so hard to commit to days one and two that I do not want to do those ever again. I still have the thoughts and the notions but I feel they are mostly theoretical, not realistic options. I've come so far now, I don't want to throw it all away for a glass of wine and everything I know it will bring.

My Weight and Diet.

I have not lost weight in the last two years but I have had many holidays and social events at which I've enjoyed beautiful food, desserts and quite a lot of chocolate. Despite this, I have not gained weight either and my eating pattern is more stable. There is not the feast and famine cycle which drinking wine perpetuated within me.

I ate pretty much whatever I wanted in the first six sober weeks but from then on tried to tackle my snacking. It was baby steps though: fewer cakes and biscuits, more of the healthy stuff to start with and trying to eat only when hungry, rather than treating it as a pleasant way to pass time when I'm at a loose end. I am still a work in progress and was reassured by a sign I read recently stating 'Of course I'm not perfect! I'm not finished yet!'.

At the time of writing I have started a meal replacement diet in an attempt to reboot my eating and satiety centres and get them functioning physiologically again. They were hijacked by the big empty hole left by booze; the emotional mayhem causing them to frantically over react and neglect their prime role of regulating appetite.

Sleep and tiredness.

In the early weeks of sobriety I was sleeping very well but despite this remained incredibly tired throughout the day. I enjoyed feeling properly tired and going to bed early, happy to have survived another sober day, and knowing I would sleep soundly.

I noted two extreme examples of my energy. One was that I could wake up after eight or nine hours sleep still being so tired that my limbs felt weak. The other was documented as 'technicolour days' when I had been Mrs Motivation herself, buzzing around all day feeling invincible and 'getting stuff done'. Finding out that all of a sudden I *could* be bothered was a hugely satisfying feeling after months or years of procrastinating over the smallest tasks which were not booze related. This activity brought such a welcome tiredness.

Paracetamol.

I no longer stock pile this drug, scared one morning I will wake up and it will not be within reach in my bedside drawer. I don't need it on a regular basis any more although I do still take it when I have a deserving headache. That I continue to get headaches at all seems incredibly unfair, but that's life I guess.

In summary, the first six weeks free from alcohol did not cause me to miss out on anything and much of life was very much better. I must be honest here though: however positive these changes were, my life was not by any means transformed to being one great bundle of laughs all of a sudden. Just because I stopped drinking, my other pre-existing problems remained, unsolved.

I imagine this to be the type of disappointment felt by those who lose incredible amounts of weight: after losing a life changing amount of weight, they find their lives are still not perfect. Everything else is exactly the same, only now they are thin. I am still very irritable, easily annoyed and short tempered.

I was always this way and while I think drinking amplified these negative features of mine and made me care very little about venting these traits, many other things that elicit the same responses from me remained. Becoming sober had not magically bestowed upon me the perfect personality. It had, however, allowed the raw materials to be identified in their true unadulterated form.

I do not really have a plan for that yet, other than learning to accept exactly who I am and acknowledging that I am still far from perfect. There is no doubt however, about the fact that I no longer drink. This is a change I have effected, which was not easy and of which I am very proud. It feels great to be able to say 'I don't drink' with conviction and sincerity and no one can take that away from me no matter how bad tempered I am.

Chapter 11 The Cinema

OH and I go out together once per month. We usually have no imagination and go for a meal and then onto the cinema. Or go to the cinema followed by a meal.

We did this one weekend recently. The 'then and now' aspect is not particularly exciting nor profound but it does highlight how difficult and complicated drinking alcohol seems to make even the simplest decisions. Going to watch a movie is an activity that precludes an evening of drinking so I would put my best efforts into minimising the extent of this.

Then

I would plan ahead for the date night on Saturday.:OH plays golf early on Sunday and often doesn't drink beforehand, he can drive, I can drink. If he is drinking (too) we do a car to cinema, car to restaurant, leave car at restaurant, taxi home. Trip to collect car next day. Then there is the order of the evening. Cinema first then dinner, means either no drink until about 8.30pm, too late, or very early drinks about 5pm before cinema, with the evidence cleared away before the babysitter arrives, followed by an unwelcome enforced break from alcohol while the film is on.

We get to restaurant and I immediately order a large glass of wine. I worry about finishing it at a time the waiter is not around to bring another one swiftly. With little babysitting time left, it's all a bit of a rush, drinking two large glasses along with dinner, and I do not feel relaxed at all.

When we get home I want to keep drinking, and do so while OH is having coffee and a biscuit before bed. I am feeling guilty about having more to drink, because, well why would you at that point in the evening?

The other option of dinner followed by cinema is no better: there is a rush to drink lots of wine before movie starts, annoyance that the movie interrupts the flow of wine, and difficulty concentrating on the film and staying awake throughout.

I feel awkward re-starting to drink after a two hour hiatus towards the end of the evening, when normal people are having coffee and biscuits before bed.

The following day I am a bit hungover, low of mood, craving of food and irritable looking after the kids.

Needless to say, I cannot be bothered to do anything.

Now

We drive to the cinema, it doesn't matter which one of us drives but usually it's OH as he gets nervous not being in control when I'm driving! I'm happy to remain a passenger. I look forward to the night as one where drinking or not is not an issue for me: any food we have will be swift and functional rather than detailed and lingering when I tend to find the lack of wine incredibly stark.

I look forward to and enjoy the film, giving it my full concentration; neither desperately trying to stay awake nor being distracted by thoughts of my next drink (or heaven forbid, if I'll even get another drink that night!).

At home there is no inebriation to hide from the baby sitter and I can chat normally, without trying to get rid of her as quickly as possible. I make tea and have biscuits without wondering if it is too late to be having another drink or if OH is going to ask why I'm having another drink at this time. I go to bed reflecting on the film, whether happy or sad, feel content and ready for a good nights sleep.

The next morning I feel great and buzz around the house in full productive mode. I feel more than great, there is an additional glee as I think how lucky I am to have enjoyed a night out without counting the cost, there being no 'price to pay' the next day and no need to declare 'that it was worth it'. It is as if my night out has come with a bonus prize.

Nothing can ever be worth feeling as bad as I did on the morning after the average low key night before. Life seems simple now. Fun with no down side. A win-win situation that I just took a while to recognise as such.

Chapter 12 Party Season

Then

Party season is coming, and many put any abstemious intentions safely aside until January. I was no different. It is so difficult to stop or even moderate a drinking pattern in December with so many parties and events taking place. I firmly believed these events prevented me exerting any measure of self-control over what I drank. I couldn't moderate how often I drank or how much I drank. Each party would offer lots of booze and I would be mandated to drink as much as possible for as long as it continued to flow. It seemed crazy not to; here was a legitimate ready made event providing an opportunity to drink to excess. The kind of events I spent the rest of the year trying to manufacture. Getting drunk was good, so getting more drunk more often must be better, right? Besides, getting drunk was practically unavoidable at this time of year. Any over indulgence was hardly my fault.

The notion of partying without drinking was ludicrous. Nowhere near my radar. Drinking was the whole point of these get togethers! I had not yet considered the option of less being more or that there could ever be too much of a good thing.

My drinking did not worry me. What worried me was the number of parties I had to go to, especially those on consecutive nights. I could not get completely thrashed every night nor could I moderate or prevent myself becoming too drunk after the first drink took my caution and threw it to the wind. This unpredictability of the night ahead excited me and scared the wits out of me simultaneously. I would plan for the worst case scenario: plenty of cash and a single front door key. The less to lose the better. I did not consider the less tangible losses I would suffer: I danced truly as if no one was watching, firmly believing I was quite good at it. I ached to have people marvel at how I had it all: the dress, the job, the family, and the sassiness to be able to let my hair truly down and relax to the point of excess outside of the boardroom. I coveted approval and sought confirmation I was holding it all together admirably.

I worried I would not be able to fulfil my minimum commitments the next day and I worried about how I would do it all again only a few hours later. I worried about being frazzled by the time Christmas arrived and managing to combine the celebrations with the many other expectations of a working mum in the month of December.

I worried a lot.

I coped by being incredibly selfish. Our normal household equilibrium was no doubt thrown off balance as the more of the mundane was left to OH. He never complained. Never suggested I did not go out, or that I take it easy, or came home earlier. I think he was almost glad that he wasn't expected (or even invited) to accompany me. I could not have OH spoiling my freedom. I never considered he might be embarrassed to be out with me!

The next day I felt I had to claim how brilliant the night had been to justify the work I had left him to cope with and the efforts he had made. I would smile dreamily and say I was glad I had gone, how I would have been notable by my absence and that I was a bit tired due to the late night.

OH either trusts me implicitly or does not care about me at all. I truly think he trusted me, still trusts me and it did not cross his mind I could have been up to no good or very close to being so. Even the time he texted me at 2.30am asking if I was okay, his main motive was concern, having woken up and realised I still was not home. I had moved onto a 'casino' because the night was still young when the party ended. It was really only a bar with no windows or clocks; easy to get into but very difficult to find any cue to leave. Being called a casino, and having a card table in the basement, justified it staying open all night and could make it appear as if drinking was not the only activity on offer. Yes, gambling sounded a much more legitimate option.

And then

I continued to be amazed at how unimportant parties became to me when I stopped drinking. All those years before, when I went to the ends of the earth to swap shifts, get a babysitter, a taxi, the next day off, a new dress and it all seemed of the utmost importance to be 'just right'.

I am no longer so desperate to go to my usual parties, with the usual gang, and I am surprised by this. I don't particularly want to go to the department's annual piss up and show what a great laugh I am and I don't really want to chat with these colleagues over loud music when I can do it on a daily basis in the coffee room, but I feel the need to show face.

I am pleased to make my excuses and leave early, escaping home in my car. I can only conclude that previously it was attractive to me as there was a group out to get drunk that I could join in with. Maybe I wanted to show I could be someone different out of the workplace? Someone more likeable? Maybe I wanted to make a certain impression?

Why would I do that? Now I can't think why I felt the need to do any of that. I'm so much less concerned about what people think of me, good or bad, and I'm moving away from needing continual reassurance that people like me. Being sober is a continual journey of reflection and self discovery. It never fails to surprise me. Yet there is no other explanation for no longer wanting to go to events I previously thought of as the highlight of the year, defined by the heavy drinking opportunities they offered.

This year I forgot to request the party night off and when I checked the rota, I was surprised to find I was not down to work on the evening. Instead, I had a long shift on the Saturday following the Friday night. This was not a problem as I knew I would be fully able to drive and work the morning after. There had been no need to request the remainder of the weekend off to recover from a monster Friday night.

Now

This year, on the Friday night I had two options and I chose the more demure. Shunning the work do, I signed up for the 'Christmas tapas quiz night', arranged by our Spanish teacher for the class. We are a mixed bunch and have known each other for over a year. I offered to drive and I enjoyed the quiz, the socialising, and just getting out of the house!

I enjoyed getting to know the others and the teachers better and quite frankly, that was enough. Even if it had turned out to be awful, I knew I could get into my little car and leave early.

I don't think my changing mindset is purely an age thing either as younger sober bloggers report the same change in interests. Whatever the reasons for my changing ways I'm looking forward to my Christmas preparations not being impeded by alcohol or hangovers, not blighted by queueing for taxis in the cold, or by the continual effort of buying and chilling and having 'enough' wine in stock over the festive period.

One of the worst aspects of Christmas drinking for me was during 2012 when I was unable to have a night off drinking. I watched OH 'having a break' or 'giving it a rest' every couple of nights, pacing himself, but I was on conveyor belt and could not, would not, did not want to step off for any time at all that could be spent drinking. Every day presented a drinking opportunity and I took them all, without exception. It was a relief when finally, on 31st December, I was back at work thus sobriety ensured. I had neither the inclination nor the ability to do this of my own volition.

I only need to glance back to this period to confirm that alcohol is nothing to celebrate, it is not a treat, and it most certainly did not enhance my life.

Chapter 13 A Stressful Day

When I reached five weeks alcohol free I had a very difficult day at work. It was a day I knew would be stressful: busy, tight deadlines, a rush to put out work that was not polished to my usual standard. There was a lot to get through, pressure of time and I felt harassed in a noisy office that made it difficult to concentrate. On top of everything, I was acting in a new team leader role and wanted to convey a confidence and capability I did not feel.

I was confident I wouldn't drink before or after that day, but was acutely aware that I was without my usual prop: it was a time I previously handled by drinking to excess.

This time I had to sit with the unpleasant feelings and emotions, feeling my way, just getting through each moment and acknowledging to myself that it was hard.

Then

Anticipating the challenge ahead, I would blot out my anxiety the night before with a bottle of wine. Unable to sleep, I would be up early and arrive at work first, as planned. I would be immediately grumpy, complaining about anything and everything not yet in place (often the IT guy who sets up the laptops for everyone but does not start work until after we do, or at the administrative staff who hadn't booked any coffee for the morning because 'they didn't know if I wanted it'). I would be overwhelmed by the stressors and cope with the workload and the hangover with a continual stream of cakes and biscuits, the peaks and troughs of a sugar frenzy exacerbating, and perpetuating the stress.

I would arrive home wound up tightly, in need of release. Immediately I would open wine and be unable to relax enough to talk about anything until I was at least half way through the bottle. Looking back OH must have realised I needed this; he never prompted me for details of my day before I started the conversation.

Once I started I was unable to stop either talking or drinking, for the rest of the evening. As the stress gradually dissipated I'd begin to look forward to my day off the following day. I'd 'fall asleep' on the sofa at 9.30pm, get up to go to bed at 11pm and be up at 3am to go to the loo and get a drink of water.

The next day would see me feeling down and hungover. I could not be bothered to do much and I'd keep going, munching excessively and mumbling and grumbling throughout the day until it was time to open the wine again.

And then

The night before my big day at work, I was feeling anxious; an understatement if ever there was one. Only part of it was to do with the task ahead, the rest was due to fear of having to get through it all without soothing my nerves with alcoholic reassurance that it would all be fine (or to forget that it may not be), or reward myself with alcoholic praise for getting through the day.

That night I hardly slept a wink and got up at 5.30am, exhausted and starving hungry. I had time and appetite for a large breakfast before work. I did feel stressed and under pressure the whole day, but I was able to deliver while remaining civil to everyone, and avoided displays of harassed hysteria and over reaction to minor problems.

I got home exhilarated and hyper, acutely aware of how much I wanted wine to calm me down and help me bask in the afterglow of success but thought 'No. I'm going to have to deal with this some other way. I'm not going to drink and it's going to be hard'.

I changed out of my work suit into comfy clothes and lay down on my bed for 15 minutes, trying to relax while OH cooked dinner. Even if I didn't succeed in relaxing very much I felt pleased I had made this change to my routine, was out of the kitchen, away from the fridge and had at least tried to relax.

As I ate dinner, I forced myself to talk about my day. It came out as more of a rant than anything else and when our dinner was over I left OH to sort out the kids while I drank tea and ate a fair bit of chocolate. I acknowledged this was a comfort response; one I was using to try to fill the hole left by wine but did not dwell upon this. One step at a time and all that.

I remained agitated all evening. It is hard to describe accurately but I felt 'antsy', unsettled, irritable but for no specific reason and 'edgy' but not in the fashionable meaning of the word! At 9pm I went to have a bath. Alas no face pack despite them appearing to be in vogue when giving up any vice!). I forced myself to start reading a novel and went to bed straight after.

I was exhausted after all the adrenaline of the day and I had a brilliant nights sleep. The next day I felt pleased with myself. I was still very hungry and ate more than I planned to, but did not binge in the same way as when coping with a hangover. I remained motivated and productive.

I had another similar day looming and still felt in need of wine. Again I used my regular mantra; saying to myself that I can have wine again if I really want to, just not tonight. If the feeling is still so prominent a full day from now, I can reconsider my options when that time comes but tonight, I will not drink. (I may need a few more baths and could well end up as a shrivelled prune at this rate!)

In short, winding down is a challenge. I've not yet found a replacement for wine in that regard. It is hard but drinking is not the way out. In fact, dealing with the fall out from drinking is probably harder than not drinking at all. I'm sticking in through these tough couple of days, trusting those who assure me it gets easier with time.

Now

Stresses at work still come fairly regularly but do not cause me nearly so much angst. Perhaps this is because I am two years older and two years more experienced at work or in some part due to the fact that I can anticipate stress, make a plan for each eventuality and thus feel capable of dealing with additional problems should they arise. I am relaxed and in many ways care much less about my performance and the perception others have of me. It all seems so much less of a big deal.

Each event seems less stressful and more manageable than before. It feels contained and I am able to define it accurately and plan it for specifically and prospectively, with rationale and clarity, as opposed to screaming 'Aaaaarrrrggghh' and delving in to a bottle of wine, while crossing my fingers, hoping I would muddle through the day and get there in the end.

Suddenly I feel very mature.

Chapter 14 A Glorious Evening

I love those days when you leave work slightly early, especially during the spring and summer months when it is gloriously sunny and relaxes into a long, warm evening.

On one such day, I stopped at a gift shop to buy a birthday present for a friend. I saw those personalised wine glasses, the ones with the little trinkets attached to the stem and a catchy phrase emblazoned around the glass. I've always liked them and hankered after my own special (wine) glass. I bought one for my friend, but resisted treating myself also. Combined with the sunny evening and early finish my thoughts then stayed on the subject of wine and conjured up a 'Wouldn't it be nice' argument, the kind that tempts me back.

Next I went to the supermarket and bought ginger beer, then went home without further ado. There I had to stop, sit down, and think hard. I had to play this movie all the way to the end in a fashion similar to that of Gwyneth Paltrow in 'Sliding Doors', noting how split second decisions have long term consequences. Did I really want what would inevitably happen if I allowed myself just one glass?

Then

I would arrive home and open a bottle of wine. So far, nothing startlingly different. As I sit to savour it (and inevitably be disappointed at its taste) I delay putting my healthy dinner on to cook as planned, (jacket potato, salad and tuna) and enjoy the effect of the wine heightened by an empty stomach.

After the first glass, the sugar in the wine has robbed me of my appetite and my good intentions, leaving me with a laissez-faire attitude. I miss out dinner, and instead have more wine and munch on a packet of crisps while basking in my sun lounge.

I savour those few minutes alone, knowing that with the passing of each minute, there is less time until my son will run back in from playing outside and the tranquility will be gone (along with half the bottle). I'm ashamed I will resent him interrupting me and my time in the world of wine.

Half drunk and brought back to the reality of domestic life, I will then be irritable doing the chores: making packed lunches and preparing school bags in a haze of booze hoping, against the odds, that I will be able to re-capture the peaceful moment once everything is done. This will not be until around 8.30pm by which time the sun will have gone down, my mood will have gone down, and of course, the bottle will have gone down too.

When the wine runs out, I'll begin drinking gin and tonic until bedtime. I will have many snacks in that time because I had no dinner. So that's allowed.

I sleep poorly and the next day will cancel my gym appointment (despite still having to pay due to the short notice). Instead I go to Weight Watchers (being so dehydrated means I weigh 'light') first thing, before eating crap for the rest of the day.

I am left feeling distended, despondent and deserving of something to cheer myself up, or to allow me to forget my troubles. This calls for a repeat glass of wine in peace and quiet in the early evening sunshine and deciding not to have dinner after all those earlier snacks...

And then

As the weeks passed I became acutely aware of this trigger and could not deny the sequence of events that would follow if I popped the cork, knocking the first domino over and setting off the cascade. I may want one glass of wine but I do not want the tidal wave of consequences that come too. Luckily this time I got out of shop quickly enough before I could begin debating the pros and cons of buying wine.

At home I address my hunger straight away by preparing and eating my healthy dinner as soon as possible. Afterwards I have cup of tea and a not-so healthy bar of chocolate (unable to choose between a Twix and a Twirl, I am not satisfied until I've had both, oh dear). As I sit in the sun eating chocolate I think about how good I will feel the following day if I stay strong and get a little further along my alcohol free journey. I try to unravel why it is that I am so brainwashed into thinking of a glass of wine as such a 'nice thing to do' when the same me knows that in reality, it brings much more than what I wish for, most of which is not very nice at all.

Writing it down always helps. It looks very easy written down: don't drink. Simple, yet in reality it remains oh so hard. Every day is a challenge but one that I do believe is worth fighting for. This alone keeps me alcohol free, just for tonight

Now

The immediate association of a sunny late afternoon and drinking wine has almost gone. At times it appears fleetingly as a 'How funny that I used to think...' type of thought but is quickly dismissed by the real me, who knows that first and foremost it is not thirst quenching and is certainly not a treat nor a kind thing to do for myself.

Instead I feel happy the sun is shining and look forward to one of my refreshing go to drinks. At first I needed a drink with a strong taste and I was rewarded by discovering ginger beer and lime. I loved the tangy after taste and it felt like a good sturdy drink. Other times (notably when bowling) I have revisited pints of soda and lime; that drink we used to mock as students as being a child-like beverage, drunk only by those who did not know how to enjoy themselves.

I still have not tried alcohol free wine or low alcohol beer. If I'm honest it's because I'm scared. Scared I will get the taste for it and a craving for the real thing will be upon me before I can say 'No, I don't drink'. I also subscribe to the opinion that alcohol, or anything pretending to be alcohol, does not taste nice! Perhaps I am lucky in that I feel immune to peer pressure and feel no need to blend in by having a pretend alcoholic drink. I don't think I felt this self assured about not drinking at first.

I drink masses of sparkling water. Masses. So much so that my usual diet coke treat now tastes horribly artificial and sweet. Only very recently, I was served sparkling water in a large wine glass, my favourite type of old, a heavy one that fits snugly in my palm, filling my hand.

I smiled as I looked at the glass; I had been scared that holding a wine glass would somehow blur the boundary between alcoholic and soft drinks that I now hold firm in my mind. My fears were unfounded though. I enjoyed holding it, topping it up, hearing the clink of ice cubes and seeing the slice of lemon bobbing around. I enjoyed the drink for what it was rather than what I hoped it would do for me. That, is what feels like a treat.

Chapter 15 The One Day Event

I was 28 days free from alcohol, my longest ever period of abstinence when I had to go to a conference in Edinburgh. It was only for a single day and consisted of the meeting, followed by drinks with colleagues, then dinner with a few of them, before returning home the same day. The sensible way to make this journey is by train. Getting to the train station however, posed some considerations.

Then
I had a dilemma. Should I take the sensible option and drive to the station and leave my car there? This meant I couldn't drink or I could have one and feel even more deprived. Either way I wouldn't enjoy the after-meeting part of the day. Option two was to take taxis to and from the station at a cost of £40, enabling me to fully partake in the evening bonding over drinks session.

This had been my usual choice in the past. I would spend the day willing the conference to be over just to get to the pub. I'd be quickly annoyed at our group wandering around looking for a specific type of pub that would not offend anyone. Personally I would have gone to the first pub we passed and since then was lamenting the diversion which was delaying my first drink and reducing the subsequent time available for drinking.

I would spend lots of money in the pub, often buying an additional round out of turn to ensure I was never left with an empty glass. I worried it would be left too late to decide who was buying the next round as the bar became busier and the drinks arrived more slowly. No wonder I became everyone's best friend.

Conversationally I would be hyper: excited to be at the beginning of an evening of drinking, relieved that a pub had been found. With drinks finally bought, the tension of waiting for that first drink which had built up all day, would fade away leaving me talking, drinking, talking, drinking, befriending those who seemed quieter, finding common ground, offering to take on projects left right and centre and whipping out my diary to pin down a date for various 'we must catch up sometime' nights out. I became louder as the time passed and bottles were emptied. Later I would wonder if I had dominated the conversation to the point of arrogance. What had people thought of me?

When the time came to move on, I wanted a brisk walk to the nearest restaurant without any hovering outside, looking at menus or trying to get a consensus from a large group of people who had not booked a table anywhere. My plan was to get seated and immediately order a bottle of wine before the waiter turned away to get the menus.

I always chose the lowest calorie options from the menu, food was not the issue here and I would not waste calories on it nor want anything too heavy. I just needed something to make it look as if I was having dinner.

As the restaurant closed and we were asked to leave, I would stumble to the station. If a train was imminently leaving I would opt to wait for the one after and spend the time in the bar having another drink. (Drinking alone is okay in a train station, isn't it?) I would buy some snacks for the train home, being starving hungry by this time having had only a measly salad earlier. My snacks varied but were not of the healthy wholesome variety.

After the train and taxi home it was often late, around 11.30pm when I arrived home wondering if it was acceptable to have more wine at that time of night? I would explain to OH that I had only had a couple in the pub, which was still really 'work' and now I needed a drink to relax at the end of a long day.

Usually, after seeing I had arrived home safely he would quickly declare he was going to bed. Perfect. Peace and privacy for another couple of hours. Throwing caution to the wind I would open a bottle of wine. I would deal with the hangover tomorrow. Who cared if I had already had enough? Nothing was going to change my plan at this stage.

And then

Desperate to remain alcohol free just a bit longer than my 28 day record, I viewed my car as a fail safe technique to remain so. It was no longer a nuisance out to spoil my fun and I chose it as the sensible option one to get to and from the station.

Throughout the day I noted how many references were made to alcohol and the over-indulging that would take place later. The first one was made during the opening remarks of the conference!

After the conference, having stayed, unusually, for the last session too, I enjoyed our 20 minute walk in the fresh air as we meandered around an unfamiliar area to find a pleasant looking pub. Still, I was first to the bar and bought everyone a drink. One colleague expressed dismay at my diet coke and asked whether he could buy me a proper drink next round. I smiled and said I had the car waiting for me back at the station.

I relaxed after the first drink, even although it was non-alcoholic. Perhaps I had less tension, less to worry about and was purely relaxing after a long day? Perhaps alcohol need not feature so critically in doing so?

I had three diet cokes in fairly quick succession. Talking a lot makes me thirsty and I had felt sleepy during the lectures. I didn't feel guilty about drinking so quickly or ordering a large one or having the next one waiting for me before I'd finished the first.

I enjoyed watching the others drink alcohol and couldn't help but compare them to a little group of drug addicts taking their drug: they had security in numbers, spoke of joining each for a shot or a nip, agreeing to try a new variety. It sounded almost sinister, not quite cult like but definitely a language common to a group of like minded individuals and you were either with them or not.

I was happy at the suggestion to walk further to a nicer restaurant. I ordered all three courses: smoked salmon starter, followed by trout, rounded off with bramble and toffee crumble and ice cream, served with a cup of tea.

I had an enjoyable chat with one friend and felt I was a much better listener. I felt calmer and paid more attention to what she said rather than waiting to talk again when she had finished. I remember all we spoke about.

I got to the train station and hopped on the train immediately. I had brought a book along and spent an indulgent hour absorbed in it on the way home.

It was yet another 'first'; the type of encounter heavily associated with booze and one in which I thought booze played an integral part. And honestly? The evening was much the same without the booze. All the positives remained yet all of the negatives disappeared. How had I not seen this before?

Now

When events like this one crop up now, my default is to take the car. Partly it avoids having to explain why exactly I'm not drinking and also it is much more convenient than public transport and travelling very easy.

Similarly, some evenings when I have work commitments I take the car and feel pleased that I am not losing out on my drinking time because of this meeting nor am I paying out a small fortune on taxis so that I can drink at them. I have no resentment about evening commitments yet similarly I do not mind if a social night is arranged and I genuinely cannot make it.

There may be a tiny part of me that misses drinking and being part of that culture but it is only a tiny part that I miss and I am glad I am no longer encumbered by the fall out it causes. The part I miss is the pure drug taking aspect of drinking: ingesting a substance to alter my state of mind. I enjoyed the feeling of becoming drunk: the loosening, both physical and emotional and the dreamy, blurry feeling that only pauses momentarily, like a roller coaster at the top of the final descent, before it hurtles downwards gaining speed and momentum until it burns itself out. Admitting I enjoyed the drug taking aspect of drinking is a scary thing to say. It makes me realise how close 'drinking too much too often' is to being 'addicted to drugs', much too close for comfort.

For now my car is my saviour. It keeps me sober when there is drink around. It keeps me warm when it's cold outside. It waits patiently for me after the last train has gone. We spend much more time together now and I'm sure it is pleased to be back in favour and no longer considered the bane of my life.

Chapter 16 Regrets

Even after the hangover of my 40th party receded, I still was not ready to confront the drinking issue and my life continued as before with me drinking a bottle of wine nearly every night, sometimes more.

My next regret came along shortly afterwards. I was writing thank you notes for all the presents I had received and also a note to the manageress of the venue. She was a mature lady and did things properly. She had done an excellent job and stage managed the evening to perfection. I really wanted to convey my sincere thanks for a job well done. Credit where credit is due and all that.

It was the end of the evening, I was tired, the wine was almost finished and the letter I wrote to her was a messy scribble of random platitudes, put together with little thought and even less planning. My writing was barely legible, the lines sloped down the page and my sentences were increasingly crammed together as I neared the bottom of the page.

I wrote a thank you note to the wife of a colleague who had given me a luxurious, quintessential bar of soap; the type I would admire on a shelf and perhaps covet before baulking at the price. I was genuinely grateful to have received the gift. I was also drunk when I wrote her a gushy note in the same scrawled hand writing, claiming delight at being introduced to such a luxury brand. On and on I went about how sure I was it would change my life now that I had appreciated the quality first hand.

It was a bar of soap for heaven's sake!

I could not be bothered to re-do this or any other letters. I wanted the task done and dusted so I continued to address the envelopes and stick on the stamps.

To my credit I did send thank you letters but I felt I let myself down by the poor quality of them. Full of verbal hyperbole, exaggerated to the extent of sounding insincere, flippant perhaps. I remain embarrassed when I think back, particularly to those ones in which I cannot remember what I wrote.

Sometimes the little things really do matter.

Chapter 17 The Last Train Home

One evening, we were out as a family at a show in the city centre. Unusually for us, we had used public transport to avoid parking issues at the large busy venue. Our journey home required us to travel on two trains; one into the central station, followed by a second out to our home area. With the crowds and queues being what they were, so it happened that we caught the Last Train Home.

Being in Central Station in Glasgow late at night is an experience. As we waited on the concourse for our platform to be announced, I could tell it was late. The dark sky was visible through the perspex roof, neon signs appeared with notifications and warnings and carts zoomed round doing errands, their orange lights flashing loudly as they sped around eerily, almost silent. There was a busy hush to the place, broken only by random shouts from groups of youths in various states of jubilation, conflict and drunkenness. It brought back memories of the last time I caught this same last train home. While this evening I noticed and detested the smells: booze, fast food and the great unwashed, the previous time I was much less aware of such nuances. Dangerously so.

Then

I had arranged to meet a friend, Susan, in the city centre as it was a mutually convenient location. We arrived on different trains from different directions and would travel home this way too.

We were no longer particularly close friends, but had been once in our university years and we now kept in touch by meeting once or twice a year. I enjoyed her company and hey, it was always another excuse to have a boozy night out.

After having a large glass of wine at home, I met her in a wine bar where, throughout the evening, we consumed two bottles of wine and a few scant, over priced but artistically presented snacks. Susan drinks very little most of the time and that night was no exception. I usually drank quite a lot and did so that night too. I had the lion's share of both bottles of wine.

At 11pm we headed back to the station and went our separate ways. There was no time to nip to the station bar and the sensible me thought this was just as well as I had had a busy day at work and was tired.

Once the train left the station, I must have dozed off near the beginning of the journey home. I awoke, startled, after a couple of stops and noticed the ladies opposite me looking at me sympathetically and smiling. They must know I work long hours I thought, they know what it's like to be so tired you can sleep anywhere. So, in order to confirm their thoughts I stretched and yawned, remarking on how exhausted I was, always on the go, busy working mum burning the candle at both ends. You know how it is, we've all been there.

The train reached their stop shortly afterwards and they alighted, leaving me in the carriage alone. The rhythmic movement of the quiet, warm train on the tracks quickly caused me to doze off again.

This time when I woke up the train had stopped. All was quiet. There was no one around and all the train doors were open. Strange, I thought. Groggy from sleep, I stood up to go and investigate. When I got out onto the platform.I realised the train had reached the end of the line, two stops past my station. It being the last train it was now finished for the night and was in the carriage graveyard until morning.

I walked up to the driver's cab at the front of the train, and was flooded with relief when I saw he was still there. With a massive effort I tried my best to look sober and apologetic, trying to muster some self respect.

'Hi, I think I've missed my stop. Can you drop me off there on your way back?' I asked as if this was an unremarkable request.

No, he could not. The train was not making any more journeys that night. The timetable was complete.

I was alone and drunk in the middle of nowhere, after midnight, with no idea how to get home.

Thankfully, only a few seconds later the driver appeared to change his mind and though clearly still angry, told me to get back in the carriage, raging and gesticulating about the trouble he would be in if he was found out. I did as he said without contemplating his motives.

I suspect he felt vulnerable alone, open to accusations from a drunk girl, and was grateful for the protection afforded by his cabin. Perhaps he felt sorry for me. Either way he drove the train back to my station. I fought to keep my eyes open this time and got out of the train as quickly as I could. He pulled away again, heading back to the end of the line, without so much as a wave or a glance in my direction.

I called a taxi to take me home from the station and waited in the cold, dark, windy car park while it arrived.

I got home and paid the fare without further incident. My usual munchies appeared on cue and mindlessly, I ate a vast amount of breakfast cereal before staggering upstairs to bed trying to cause minimal disruption to the rest of the household.

Finally, I hunkered down under the duvet, trying to warm up and hide from the inevitable monster hangover that was on its way. I closed my eyes in the hope that the events would cease to exist, and it would all simply go away.

Was it worth it? What do you think? Needless to say my lasting memory of that night was not the chat I had with Susan. That earlier enjoyment had been eclipsed by the drunken drama which followed.

Now

As the four of us stood together on the concourse, I counted my blessings that I was not in a similar state to time before. I was pleased to be clear, alert, aware of the crowds, pick pockets, undesirables. I was a little cold and impatient for the train to arrive but I had my wits about me and could keep myself and my children safe and shielded from any mishaps.

I enjoyed the atmosphere: people still buzzing and excited from the show, kids as high as kites at being up so late and having such a wild adventure and I felt so lucky that I was aware of these things. I felt glad I had enjoyed the evening without lamenting it was an outing which precluded my daily wine intake and I felt reassured that when I became angry with the kids, it was fully justified and did not reflect either my being drunk and irrational, or not drunk enough and irritated at not being able to drink more.

Basically, it was better and I had a sudden rush of positive re-enforcement. Yes, I have looked longingly at the odd glass of wine over the summer and yes, at times I have felt deprived. Yet these instances are almost insignificant compared to the gains an alcohol free life keeps delivering. When I look back at this and other 'thens', I realise that the odd lovely glass of wine always leads straight back to the same destructive misery at the end, no exceptions.

I felt a true physical tiredness. It made me happy and I looked forward to going home to bed, to sleep, knowing I would be able to do so without any drama, embarrassment, loss of respect, episodes of bingeing or with a price to pay the next day.

Most importantly, we all have memories of that show, the whole evening's events and the children often talk about it. I'm grateful I didn't spoil it for myself or anyone else by trying to shoe horn wine into an evening which needed nothing even pretending to improve it. This night is another I will recall when I am tempted in future.

evening, we were out as a family at a show in the city centre. Unusually for us, we had used public transport to avoid parking issues at the large busy venue. Our journey home required us to travel on two trains; one into the central station, followed by a second out to our home area. With the crowds and queues being what they were, so it happened that we caught the Last Train Home.

Being in the central train station in Glasgow late at night is an experience. As we waited on the concourse for our platform to be announced, I could tell it was late. The dark sky was visible through the perspex roof, neon signs appeared with notifications and warnings and carts zoomed round doing errands, their orange lights flashing loudly as they moved around, eerily silent. There was a busy hush to the place, broken only by random shouts from groups of youths in various states of jubilation, conflict and drunkenness. It brought back memories of the last time I caught this same last train home. While this evening I noticed and detested the smells: booze, fast food and the great unwashed, the previous time I was much less aware of such nuances. Dangerously so.

Chapter 18 Discretion and Trust

I am chatty. I am more chatty with a bottle of wine inside me but since doing without, I find I am still chatty. I can talk to people, find common ground and am always able to introduce myself to new people with 'Hi, we've not met before, my name's Rachel...'. This was not second nature to me for a while but after twenty years of moving around different posts in my career, introducing myself regularly has become second nature. It is something I still do at work if I don't recognise the person I'm speaking too, so much so that I've been met with a 'Yes, we know who you are by now!' more than occasionally.

My chattiness has developed in response to the need for it to occur at times I would rather sit quietly and say nothing. I can cope in social situations and can make conversation but I view it as something that has to be done, not something I would necessarily choose to do. I am helped by the fact that I am genuinely nosey and keen to hear what others are doing. I like details and this leads to me asking lots of questions. I lack the reserved skills I see in OH and neither tact nor diplomacy are my strong points. Ever wondered if a couple have split up? Just wait while I go ask them. How did I know someone was looking for another job? Because I asked them if the rumours were true! How else?

The problem is, that armed with all this information I tend to gossip, particularly with the more newsworthy nuggets. I can grade my degree of trustworthiness. If I'm told 'This must go no further. This is serious', then I can keep my mouth shut. But in the absence of such explicit instruction I have no such compunction. Defining how I came about information and how this impacts on whether it is okay to share it is difficult and I tend not to err on the side of caution as often as I should.

Needless to say, discretion was not an attribute I had while drinking.

Then

In my previous incarnation, I really could not be trusted. The problem was that my insecurity made me try to be all things to all people, and many did trust me and told me their secrets. At work too, I held a position that came with respect and an expected degree of trust that could become blurred across professional and personal boundaries.

At times I would hear gossip and would sit thinking 'I know the next instalment of this story but I must not say'. Holding the conversational cards becomes difficult when sharing of their content is not permitted. I would be itching to tell, itching to be the centre of attention and feel important by what I could add above and beyond anyone else.

As the glasses of wine notched up I would figure a way to gain collusion and spew forth said secrets. I might start with a 'This must go no further', 'Just between you and I' or 'You didn't hear this from me' so absolving myself of sole responsibility for facilitating the exponential spread of news.

I loved sharing other peoples' secrets but it often got me into trouble. I never considered two individuals might know each other or indeed be related and I discovered that not everyone forgets everything they hear when they are drunk. Particularly not shocking, newly revealed truths. I still worry about fall out from something I have over-shared coming back to haunt me several years on. I worry about being challenged over gossiping and sharing information I received whilst in a privileged position.

The day after the night before, I would call friends on the casual pretext of asking if they had enjoyed the night and to enquire 'How's the head today?'. I hoped they would spontaneously reassure me I had done nothing terribly wrong but usually this was not forthcoming. Next I would ask who they thought was the most drunk? Were they very drunk? Was I? Did I make a tit of myself? Often the reply was 'You were in good form', 'You were such a laugh' or 'You were just enjoying yourself' which is far too vague and loaded for the paranoid drinker to interpret accurately. Lastly I would own up and come straight out with it: 'I had far too much to drink, I hope I didn't do or say anything too bad did I?'.

The sad thing is, you never really know. Those whom you ask, your friends, try to make it seem better for you and try to hide you from the truths of your behaviour by omitting the details of the true depths to which you sank.

Now

Two years sober (and older and wiser) I have learned not to trust anyone with very much at all but I have also learned that I can trust myself more reliably. I know, perhaps always knew, what bits were for public sharing and what was off limits but now I respect that distinction much more.

When I still can't quite keep a lid on the latest news I dress it up, change it beyond recognition, or attribute it to a friend that no one present knows of. Keeping secrets is still a burden and sometimes you need to share them. Realising the correct way to do so is not possible when the wine takes over control of your speech and removes the natural safeguards along the pathway from thoughts as they become words spoken aloud.

I feel I am now a better person. A good person who now deserves the privileges they are credited with. I am a better listener and a more sincere friend and confidante.

I'm relieved I no longer have to make the phone call of shame the next day or apologise for anything I may have said out of turn.

Small but significant changes are present everywhere you look when you remove the veil of alcohol from your life.

Chapter 19 Saturday Night Texting

Inappropriate communication while drunk is a hallmark of those who over do it. It has been known as 'Drink and dial' in the past and I suggest with the advances in telecommunications and social media, the same phenomenon would now be named 'Pissed and post' or 'Wrecked and text'. My drinking peaked (or sunk, depending on your point of view) when I was in the texting era.

Then

I would send texts during the evening to those who were not present, demanding that they 'Remind me to tell you what x just said or did!'. If I was drinking at home, I would be texting everyone in my message log, following up on previous discussions, making plans, suggesting ideas, all of which I felt had to be done this minute because it always seems like such a great idea, right?

If I had been out, once home again I would text everyone about what a great night we'd had, how we must catch up again and generally confess too much love for friends I did not love and sometimes for those I barely knew.

I would immediately follow up and confirm arrangements I had made hastily earlier in the evening with one of my new 'best friends in the whole world' whom I had hugged to seal our new friendship. As we chatted I would say 'You should come round for dinner one night soon, we can catch up again and the boys can meet'. We are so sure our partners will get on well together and do not for one minute consider the likelihood of this. I shudder at the number of times I have had a couple around to our home for dinner and have left the 'boys' alone to talk in the international common language of football, while we girls headed to the sunroom to share fizz, wine and gossip without interruption from the boys.

I feel sorry for OH as I put him, a naturally shy, quiet and unassuming chap into this prefabricated situation so often and left him to his own devices with someone he barely new (and was not indeed, particularly interested in meeting). These nights were perhaps always, even subconsciously, dates to allow another night of guaranteed heavy drinking, me having found a like-minded, equally paced drinking partner.

The next day I'd scroll through the lists of texts, being irritated at those who had not yet replied, identifying the worst ones to figure out a damage limitation plan and groaning inwardly as the potential fiasco added to my hangover making everything worse. Why did I say that? Did I really say that? What did I do that for? Were they as drunk as me? Why couldn't I have just waited and texted today instead of at 2am? If you receive a text at 2am it's either a true family emergency or a very drunk friend.

Next I have to decide how to carefully word my morning after texts to sound casual and breezy as if there was nothing untoward about my text(s) of the night before. The 'Hi, me again' nature, posed to provide an opening for the other to comment on the state I was in the night before, without having to ask directly and thus incriminating myself perhaps needlessly.

If they don't provide the reassuring answer I need, then I worry it was either too embarrassing for them to mention or they were also so drunk they did not notice my behaviour. I hope it's the latter but a nagging feeling that it's the former torments me nonetheless.

All in all it serves to compound my hangover, nausea, headache, irritability and darken my day even further. All this on a day when I have limited ability and am struggling to function on the most basic level. I do not need this aggravation. Why has this landed upon me too? I try to close my mind to it and put it away for another day, one when I'm feeling better.

Now

I now have time on Saturday nights (and a functioning brain) and often catch up with my phone messages from the previous week.

One recent Saturday night, I had a text conversation with a friend to arrange a walk the following afternoon. In the morning I could remember all the details of the arrangements (I hoped she could too!) and had no fears there was anything I said that I wished I could take back.

Then I replied to a some emails which had been lingering in my inbox for a few days; ones that needed a little thought and concentration. I have no need to worry that I've made a mistake, emailed the wrong person, forgotten to attach the attachments (although I forget to do that sober too), or have copied in people whom I absolutely should not have copied in. I can remember all my passwords and can shop on line or do my banking without fear of gross financial errors.

I read and commented on a few blogs. I absorbed what I was reading and made some useful (IMHO!) contributions to discussions in the comments section. Pertinent comments, appropriate comments generally free from typos, comments which had travelled the right way through the BS filter between having the thoughts and typing them out on the keyboard.

This morning I am pleased I can stand by any comments I made. They are what I really meant to say and are not glib knee jerk reactions spouted off whilst drunk. I am pleased I have no damage control to worry about. I am reassured I have not offended anyone, been inappropriate to anyone or loose tongued and gossipy at the expense of anyone.

I feel calm and relaxed. The day ahead seems simple and uncomplicated. It just 'is', without undercurrents of what ifs and what might be.

Why did I ever drink so much? What was I trying to achieve? What need was I trying to meet? I can't explain that right now as I don't know the answer. I do know, however, that I cannot do anything to change the past but I have definitely made a positive change for the future.

Chapter 20 Regrets

My last remaining grandparent died at the peak of my drinking. She was 94 years old and had suffered a long, slow, undignified death in a nursing home compounded by an awareness of her progressive dementia. Although at the end she was confused as to who exactly I was, I had been her first and favourite grandchild all my life and she made little secret of this fact.

It is a horrid thing to say, but her passing was a relief in many ways; both for her and her carers, my mother included. There was a feeling of her being released from the torment of being trapped in a body that no longer worked and of them being able to care but unable to improve her situation.

My Grandma came from a large family. She had 13 siblings and though she had outlived the majority of them, her funeral was well attended. My mother had an endless number of cousins, many of whom I had never met but had heard about in conversation over the years.

On the day of the funeral I was anxious about many things: the ad hoc child care we had arranged, how my mother would cope, how I would cope, and I looked forward to it all being over so I could collapse with a supply of wine that evening.

In Scotland, funerals are rarely dry. Indeed they are seen as an opportunity 'ta hae a gid drink' and become reacquainted with far flung members of the family.

The ceremonial parts of the day were over by 10.45am and we filed into the function suite of a nearby hotel. Tea and coffee were served initially but at 11 o'clock precisely, a member of staff opened up the bar. The usual suspects formed a queue. I stayed by my mother's side as she introduced me to her various cousins, aunts and uncles. I felt this gave her a topic of conversation without referring directly to the reason why we were congregating.

After a short while she introduced me to a lovely couple who were sat alone. We found some common ground and joined them at their table. My husband went to buy a round of drinks at the bar. Knowing of my stress, he asked me if I wanted a glass of wine. His intentions were sound.

Of course I did! Plus, I was pleasantly surprised that drinking wine before midday would not look out of place given so many others were purposefully imbibing. One glass slipped into another and I loosened up.

I morphed into party mode, suddenly becoming best buddies with friends and relatives I had only recently met. I gushed over common ground and recounted the same line of chat to each of them, the recurring theme being that the funeral was great, not in the slightest bit sad, because it had allowed us all to meet up and get to know one another. This would not have happened had my Grandma still been alive.

I spoke to one of my great aunts at lengths. She had become close to my mother during the final months of Grandma's deterioration and had lent her a great deal of support. I impressed upon her how helpful this had been to my mother, who would not voice such gratitude herself. I think I told her this three times, stressing more emphatically each time, how sincere I was and and asked her to please ensure their relationship continued despite the reason for it no longer remaining. Again I emphasised how good it was that Grandma had died this way and allowed them to build a friendship anew. Linking my arm through hers I marched us to the bar to seal the deal with a drink.

Such was the extent of my chatting, I missed the food which came and went before I had a chance to put my drink down and get something to eat. This did not help matters.

I worked the room. Introducing myself to those I didn't know and joining them for a drink. Catching up with those I did know and had not seen for years. Swapping news of careers, children, health and wealth. There was little mention of my Grandma or of any memories of her we shared.

I had no disrespectful intentions and would have been horrified had I observed myself flitting around the room through sober eyes (as I'm sure some did). But my behaviour was irreverent and inappropriate, and to this day I am ashamed of myself. This was not a reunion or a celebration. It was a solemn event, primarily to provide refreshments for mourners who had travelled some distance to pay their respects, before they made the return journey. I had hijacked it from its serene purpose and reduced it to a common piss up for one and all. My abstemious Grandma would have been disappointed, perhaps bewildered, to see her little favourite staggering around waving a wine glass less than an hour after she was buried.

No matter how long we are sober, we cannot change or erase events of the past. AA teachings suggest we make amends to those we have harmed or wronged through our drinking. Looking ahead now, it seems important not to procrastinate over this, lest you leave it too late and the opportunity to do so is missed.

Chapter 21 Christmas

As I approached my second sober Christmas, many people asked how I felt about it. I had lots of feelings, all now free to come out and make themselves known, but regarding being sober that Christmas, my overwhelming feeling was one of relief. Relief that I did not have to drink. Relief that I was free from it. Relief from the preoccupation it brought and relief from a life dominated by the associated logistics of repeatedly drinking to excess.

Then

One December, as I failed again to moderate, I was coming around to the idea that I would have to stop drinking at some point. In my wisdom I decided to make the most of it until that time arrived.

December was a great month for drinking to excess: everyone was 'partying hard' and 'hilarious' behaviour was both permitted and excused. Everything was associated with drinking alcohol. Cafes with twinkly lights enticed me in to enhance my shopping experience with a drink as darkness descended at 4pm. Putting up the Christmas tree and decorations deserved a glass of wine as a reward, if not even earlier to ease the undoubtedly stressful process itself. Catching up, visiting, socialising. These all revolved around drinking alcohol, indeed getting drunk was the only motivation for some of them. I was always up for any occasion regardless of the exact reason. If there was booze, I'd be there.

I was organised and my routine was perfected to cover all the eventualities I'd dealt with on various nights out.

My evening routine was hallmarked by the fact that I would be incapable by the end of the evening: I got cash from the machine beforehand to leave the cash card at home, took the house key off the bunch to minimise the number I could lose and had my 'party purse' which was small enough to hold rather than put down and leave behind. I pre-booked taxis. This avoided any delay to the start of the evening and ensured a ride home when my brain was not functioning sufficiently to make the call later on.

To deal with hangovers I juggled work and other commitments into suitable times to accommodate feeling fragile at others.

By Christmas eve I was exhausted. Still, I drank more wine, argued with my brother, set the world to rights with my father in a fit of 'If you can't beat 'em join 'em'. A final glass after the presents were laid out meant later to bed and a hangover guaranteed.

On Christmas morning I cranked my head gradually from the pillow as the children rushed in, full of joy and noisy excitement. I was feeling awful, rebranded for my family as 'tired' and of course guilty that I was not fully sharing their joy.

We often had house guests. I believed I deserved to drink to deal with the 'stress' of OH's extended family. I deserved to drink after the endless cooking, clearing up and changing of beds. I kidded myself that I should offer, and keep offering, alcohol to guests. Mostly his family don't drink very much but enjoy a small sherry before lunch whilst on holiday. I would join in with that too, generally having more than a thimbleful. I would then bring the wine out at lunchtime and while some would have a small amount while eating, I would continue throughout the meal, into the clearing up period and for most of the afternoon too.

I was wary of how the true extent of my drinking would be observed by our guests. I did not want them to think I was drinking too much every day and would conceal my glasses of wine and sherry within the mess of preparation in the kitchen or disguised next to unwashed glasses. I suspect I did not hide it as well as I thought.

I invited friends to our house. Usually families and usually in the afternoon both to enable an earlier start to drinking and because we all had young children. The plan would be for the children to amuse themselves and leave the adults alone, chatting and drinking. I resented the intrusion of the children each time they appeared, interrupting, needing adult input. When their bedtime came I was not particularly interested or patient, wholly focussed on continuing the drinking which, by then, had advanced beyond any boundaries.

Even when there was nothing planned, come early evening I would open another bottle of wine. A couple of times I thought to myself 'here we go again', when the first sip was a disappointment and merely reminded me of the time before when I'd had too much. But it did not make me stop or take a break. It seemed to be all I knew and there was no realistic alternative.

I could not comprehend how life could carry on at this time of year without drinking alcohol. It seemed that by removing alcohol I would ruin the rest of my life and be doomed to spend it miserable and wanting. To survive the stress of Christmas required wine. I failed to see it was the cause of the problem, truly believing it to be the solution.

So I drank every day that year. Sometimes drinking was enjoyable, sometimes it was necessary and sometimes it was for no reason. I recognised having too much of a good thing and its diminishing appeal, but my mind could not comprehend having opportunity to drink yet choosing not to do so. I went to great lengths to make it everywhere we were invited and engineered not to be the one driving following a nonchalant discussion with OH.

'Do you want me to drive?',

'I don't mind, whatever you prefer',

'I'm happy to drive',

'Okay, you drive then', knowing that OH prefers not to drink at these things as we are still parenting our children, and always prefers to drive.

As the festive period wore on I grew more and more tired, became increasingly bloated and fatter each day as my eating patterns deteriorated and the Christmas cake was put to good use. I gained weight and felt very down about that too.

I was glad to be working on New Year's Eve. It was a night to drink even more than usual and I was so hungover from the day before that I did not even want to drink at all. Working was the only thing that stopped me. But there I was grumpy and short tempered, annoyed with everything and unpleasant to work with, I suspect.

I think most of the Christmas stress and dramas I experienced were due to chronic low grade hangover symptoms. Instead of helping me cope with the demands of the festive period, the only thing made better by wine was the perpetual want and need for more and more wine.

And then

The following Christmas I was nine months free from alcohol and looking forward to the festive period without worries of enabling my drinking, hiding my drinking or suffering the hangovers from my drinking.

We put up the Christmas tree and it was notably simple and exciting for the children. There did not seem to be any of the stress or drama that I usually associated it with. I didn't mind that the decorations were mis-matched, home-made and not distributed evenly around the tree. My children had been the project managers and I was happy to observe their work.

I had been productive throughout December. I was able to make full use of my free time; no longer held back by hangovers. I decided not to go to many Christmas parties: not because I couldn't drink but because many had very little appeal when considered without the booze.

I went to a few friends' gatherings and enjoyed chatting mindfully and sincerely to others, being a good parent and considerate to my children and leaving after a short but enjoyable time. I loved that I could drive everywhere and doing so was not coupled with frustration at not being able to drink. Looking back, the reason I did not enjoy events I had previously driven to was due to an overwhelming feeling of deprivation at being *forced* to remain sober, rather than actually *choosing* to stay sober at a party. Such twisted logic was not uncommon.

We received a crate of fine wine as a Christmas gift. Six bottles of red and six white. I was dis-interested in the contents and left the box aside for a couple of days before my husband opened it and perused the selection. Twice he had wine with a meal and each time I observed his drinking behaviour. He poured the glass as the meal was being served, not before. When I looked I saw he had poured a tiny glassful. I would have been horrified if he had poured the same amount for me. We were two-thirds of the way through our meal before he took his first sip. I mean, had he forgotten it was there? He managed to finish it and progressed onto coffee with dessert. As we flopped on the sofa later he poured another, even smaller amount this time. He took a few sips over the space of an hour and then left almost an inch in the bottom of the glass: he'd had enough and did not want to finish it.

This whole attitude is unfathomable to me. Had I been drinking wine I would have poured larger glasses, earlier on, taken the bottle to the table for top-ups, shunned the coffee and dessert and continued to drink on the sofa afterwards, stopping only when I 'fell asleep'. Luckily I did not need to do this anymore and I watched him out of interest, rather than with envy or longing for wine of my own.

Unusually, we had no house guests that year and I very much enjoyed our time alone as a family. I was up bright and early on Christmas morning, sharing in the juvenile enthusiasm, no longer resentful at the early hour.

The rest of the day was lovely. It did not disintegrate as I got progressively drunk and I did not fall asleep on the sofa after lunch. There was no need to offer wine, open wine, have wine, manage wine. No concern about its continued supply or disposal. I was content to be at home, playing with the children and their new games, preparing simple meals with minimum fuss and no expectation. I did not invite families round on the pretext of catching up. The mere thought of all these visitors made me feel exhausted and filled me with dread, now that I am content with what I have, what we are.

I'm no longer hiding from reality, hiding behind the booze. I was not pre-occupied by how I was feeling each day or with what I would be drinking later. I enjoyed watching television without falling asleep or appearing rude in front of guests. I relaxed, unwound, and had a rest! I felt great and thoroughly enjoyed one of our few remaining Santa years.

Now

The next year was different again. Being sober was not so notable and had become more routine. There were no longer decisions to be made about drinking. This year we did not open any wine at all: my parents were driving (one doesn't drink, not particularly through choice and the other can't drink enough when away from home so suffers without any. And you wonder where it comes from?). My OH was truly not bothered about having any wine so chose not to. Hence, there were no drinkers at our Christmas dinner.

I have become less of the model parent as I become used to being sober all the time and take some aspects of it slightly for granted now it's my default setting. The novelty has worn off a bit and I'm no longer keen to play the childrens' games all day. I think my true colours are now visible. I like time alone to do my own pursuits. I like time to read and potter. I remind everyone that it's my holiday too and could well be considered selfish at times.

For the first time we spent New year abroad this year, to enjoy some sunshine and outdoor time. I took this in my stride; knowing it would be very different but not minding precisely which aspects of it would be different.

When drinking I would have been anxious about such a change to the usual routine. How would I fit drinking into our days on holiday, particularly when it was not a priority for anyone else? How would I ensure an uninterrupted supply of wine around foreign public holidays? What if the shops were closed? What if we decided to eat in one evening and, heaven forbid, there was no wine in the fridge?

My mind is emptied of this tortuous pattern of plotting and planning. It is free and available to engage in the present, to be open to opportunity and to go with the flow instead of trying to swim against the tide.

Chapter 22 Family Commitments

The Hallowe'en school disco is one of the most dreaded annual events. In my locality the evening involves three discos, each lasting one hour and being held consecutively between the hours of 6pm and 9.30pm. Imagine the logistic difficulties of having children of different ages attending different discos, while trying to relax and sink a bottle of wine on a Friday night.

Then

I would dread the prospect of the evening and text around the neighbours to arrange lift sharing well in advance. I would aim to do the early, 'going there' runs to bring my responsibility to an end as early as possible.

It was a race against time to get them ready and I helped with costumes and face paint through gritted teeth: why was it always such a last minute rush? Why was it always a hassle? Why was it never fun?

I feel so guilty harassing my kids to get ready and out the door that I am over generous with spending money. I dole it out, not really caring that they will rot their teeth by having an excess of the sweets and juice on sale. It's only one night, I think, yet that same thought does not apply to me; I am not prepared to miss out on drinking for even one night.

I pick up the neighbours' kids and bark at them all to get into the car and to Stop. Shouting. They are seated next to each other.

I would huff and puff through the parking scrum, the rain, the crowds. I worry only fleetingly as I sign the emergency contact form saying I am available in case of accident or injury before dismissing it as a mere formality. They never need to call us, it's only a precaution.

I note many mums are helping out at the disco. Aren't they missing wine too?

I wave the kids off into the gym hall where Cheezy Chunes are blasting out. I am annoyed by one boy who has decided he no longer wants to go in; he is scared by some of the costumes. I phone his mum to explain this before detouring on my way home to drop him off again. It takes great restraint to remain civil to both him and his mother as they delay my date with wine.

Back home, I rant about the trauma of it all, getting the wine opened as I speak. It's much later than usual, much later than I had planned and I finish the first glass before I've finish my rant.

But all too soon it is spoiled. The first wave of younger kids arrive back home. Hyperactive and high on sugar, chattering and looking for attention, in no way keen to have a quiet bath and go to bed. Despite knowing this, I try and fail to hurry them upstairs, away from me, becoming more irritated as time passes and my immersion into the peaceful world of wine is hindered by mundane banalities of life..

Now

I was aware I was 'behind' on football runs so I offered to do more than my share of the disco runs. This offer was well received by the neighbours.

I spent a hilarious twenty minutes in the bathroom bonding with my children as I attempted to make up one pirate and one bunny with Max Factor and Rimmel.

I got organised to leave in plenty time, got parked easily and joined the queue. At school I filled in the permission slips confidently with my own mobile number rather than OH's.

Now that I can be bothered with small talk, I did the social thing and exchanged pleasantries across the gym hall with other mums (many of whom are helping. I'm not, so no change there) and agree we must catch up one afternoon. My heart no longer sinks at the thought of an afternoon meeting for coffee instead of a wine o'clock meeting for booze.

Once home I have a 40 minute pit stop before I have to turn around and go back to school to pick them up, and drop off some others. Time enough for a cup of tea, a biscuit and a chat with OH.

An hour later I have another 40 minute wait and reflect upon how irritating this would be had I been wanting and waiting to settle down with wine. This time I have cup of tea and a slice of toast.

Finally I collect the 10 and 11 year old girls and am amused to listen to their chat in the back of the car (why Goths should never have a suntan and how 'annoying' it is when long dangly earrings bump into your neck!).

At home, I spend 30 minutes gently removing the bunny's pink bunny nose. (Much longer than it took to apply it. Note to self not to use Lipfinity for this again.) It takes patience, cotton wool and a combination of cleanser, eye make up remover, baby shampoo and soap to get it all off, but we get there eventually without falling out about it in the process.

That in itself is a true 'first'!

I am glad the kids enjoyed their disco. I am pleased to have been more involved with them throughout the evening, to be present and to be so willingly, not begrudgingly having forgone my nightly wine. I did the right thing and remained responsible in case of accident or injury. Doing so made me feel proud of myself yet at the same time a bit sad that staying sober for a kids' party was such a notable event for me.

Chapter 23 First day of Holidays

Then

It always began with a hangover. Drinking the night before was undeniably allowed (the official start of the holiday), required (due to the stress of packing) and usually excessive (as no work the following day).

The travelling would be tense, fraught, stressful, and I would be on edge wondering how it would all pan out, wondering how I would manage to drink that evening. Would the shops still be open when we arrived? Would there be a bar close by? Would the children need to go to bed leaving us confined within the walls of our accommodation? Yes sure, I could go over to the hotel bar, buy two drinks and bring them back to our apartment but I know OH would think this way too much hassle: he wouldn't be that desperate for a drink and would suggest we didn't bother.

I didn't want to look too desperate for a drink and was acutely aware that it would be only one drink. Only one drink. Quite frankly it was easier to deal with having no alcohol than having just one drink but still, on the first night of my holiday, I really wanted to drink.

Many of my fellow countrymen and women drink alcohol before they fly, no matter the time of day or night. It's not because they are afraid of flying. It is simply what being on holiday means to so many. It is usual to see people with pints of lager and glasses of wine at 5am in Glasgow airport. I have never done this, for several reasons really. Once I start to drink I like to continue. I don't want to be brought back down to earth and reminded of my commitments and responsibilities, particularly those associated with travelling. It is early to start drinking and I would never last the day. I would want to be left alone to 'fall asleep' in a few hours time and having two small children on a plane would not allow that. Further, I am too embarrassed to ask for alcohol on the plane. I have no objection to others drinking: I think they are on holiday and it is their choice. So what? I certainly don't think badly of them, yet I feel others would think badly of me: drinking in the morning with two small children in tow. Irresponsible with disordered priorities is what I imagine they would say. OH would be genuinely perplexed. Why was I having alcohol? Why? It is a good question to which there is no good answer. Anyhow, I didn't want to have to explain myself nor justify my actions. It was just easier not to go there.

I would arrive at our destination fraught and pre-occupied with the alcohol purchasing opportunities (or lack thereof) that would meet us on arrival. Would there be a shop? A supermarket? Would it be open? Would I be able to walk there?

Arriving in a foreign country, going to an unknown resort to stay in unseen accommodation, it now seems bizarre that it was booze at the forefront of my mind and not any other of the myriad of unknowns we faced.

Now

I look forward to our holiday looming ever closer with excitement. I have no stress or fear building as the day draws closer.

The new me is laid back about packing. What do we really need except our passports and cash? If we forget anything crucial we can always buy it there.

The duty free shop is a non-experience. I no longer have to explain why I am buying a bottle of gin (in case they don't have the right brand in Spain) when really it's to make sure there is booze immediately available wherever we end up. I don't miss the lightweight plastic bottles which feel cheap and seedy and take up the vast proportion of my hand luggage. Now I fill it with all sorts instead! Having progressed beyond mushy bananas, plastic spoons, wipes and nappies, I can now pack things for me that I have both space for in my bag and space in my head to remember. I have a kindle, a magazine, tissues, a lip salve, a bottle of water, snacks appropriate to my latest diet, a fleecy hoody for departure and sun glasses for arrival.

Such simple luxuries. Such profound content.

Chapter 24 Now

The single word I would use to describe the effect alcohol had on my daily life is encumbrance. Now that alcohol is removed I feel light and free, as if a burden or heavy load has been removed and no longer weighs me down and holds me back.

Drinking had brought me a whole set of problems, considerations, situations to be managed, plans to be made, commitments to re-prioritise and excuses to rationalise. My brain, my hard drive, had to deal with all these aspects first and foremost leaving little residual capacity to deal with the rest of life. As the drinking tumour grew, ugly and tortuous, it obliterated more and more of its environment, just as a cancer does, breaching boundaries with no respect for its surroundings.

Breaking point comes when the ability to manage life is no longer possible due to the capacity occupied and controlled by the malignancy of drinking. This is the first major crossroads.

We can choose to let our lives progressively unravel, accumulating losses and regrets and we reach the final point of no return. Or, we can take a deep breath and brave the unknown alternative, stop drinking and take back control.

This is a huge step and requires a degree of faith that all those sober people are telling the truth: that there is a huge amount of life after booze, a happy and fulfilling life with a mass of opportunity, which can be yours should you choose to take it.

Sobriety is changing. The belief of a life filled only with AA meetings, deprivation and boredom, fighting a wish to drink each day has changed. An increasing number of people are understanding the lie that is alcohol, and can now see through the facade which fooled us for so long. Choosing to become and remain free from alcohol is now a positive lifestyle choice.

In the population at large, the gradual sea of change has built up to reach the current tipping point, a point of flexion where the gathered momentum causes an exponential burst of change, the way that gradual melting of glaciers causes slow movement in the plates of the earth, until the earthquake explodes, magnifying the effect of the initial subtle change several thousand fold.

Fashions change and it is now more fashionable than ever to have it all. Really have it all. This means having it, doing it, driving home and remembering it afterwards. Looking as good at the end of the night as we did at the start. Enjoying ourselves and socialising with exotic drinks to break the ice: an electric blue mocktail is a great conversation starter with no need for the addition of mind altering substances. Having it all means being in control, taking responsibility for ourselves and the image we portray. It means leading a high quality life, the type that we really want, that others admire.

I feel fabulous when people ask why I don't drink and I can answer honestly that I no longer need to. Why would I?

****

I hope you enjoyed this book and that you will consider leaving your review on the Amazon site to share with others.

There is always more to read on my blog www.soberisthenewrachelblack.blogspot.co.uk

If you haven't read **Sober is the New Black,** an account of the ups and downs I had when I originally gave up alcohol, then read the opening chapters below.

Chapter 1. I want wine.

'What would you like to drink?'

The question hangs innocently in the air. What would I like to drink? Around me I can see cocktails being mixed at the bar, I can hear the glug glug of wine being poured at the next table and I watch someone take that first refreshing sip of beer.

I want wine. I want lots of wine. I want it quickly and I want it now while my stomach is empty and it will rapidly reach my bloodstream, quickly course to my brain and fulfill the ever-present need.

Yes, I want wine. I want wine very much, yet at the same time, I don't. Should I or shouldn't I? I want what I cannot have, yet here I am, all grown up, surely I can do as I please? I am torn between the options, exhausted by the mental gymnastics going on inside my head. This small decision of huge magnitude is the first crossroads at the beginning of my journey into the unknown. From today I am adopting an alcohol-free life. I am unsure if I can succeed, but know that failure is not an option.

How can it be so hard not to do something? Just don't do it. It should not be difficult. But it is. So, so difficult. Can I make the short term sacrifice of what I want right now, for what I want most of all? Can I bear the immediate hardship in the hope of a longer term gain? It should be a simple decision but making the correct choice is so hard.

It is 6pm and I am sitting on a beautiful terrace watching the sun set. I am on holiday. I arrived this afternoon at a luxurious all inclusive hotel in the sun. It was an early start and now I am tired and need to sleep but I am also hungry and must eat first. The restaurant opens at 7pm. There was an hour to wait when the waiter asked that simple question.

Today was to be my new start. My 48 hour hangover from the last boozy episode had receded and I felt better. I'd learnt from my mistakes and my many failed attempts at moderation. My hangover mindset had changed from never wanting to drink again to realising that I could not, must not drink again. I had come to the conclusion that becoming completely alcohol-free was the only option for me in the long term. But. I could just have one tonight. In fact, I could just drink tonight then start stopping again tomorrow. Or start stopping after the holiday. What difference would an extra two weeks make? Or would it be easier to stop once back to the routine of work and the hum drum of daily life? Probably not.

In the days prior to this holiday I had felt anxious about the lack of control I would have over my drinking in a resort with plentiful, all inclusive bars: all normal restraints absent, no driving, no work, no pub closing time. I was acutely worried that the bar service would be slow, the drinks would be small and inadequate and I'd feel embarrassed to keep asking for another. I didn't want a hangover in the baking heat the following day yet I wanted an alcoholic drink now. The two were mutually exclusive and I felt panicked by my lack of conviction.

This time was supposed to be different and failure was not an option. This time was supposed to be It, yet here I was hesitating at the first hurdle. Twice previously I had ended my attempts at abstinence when the first hurdle presented itself. A social function, a night out, a birthday, a Friday, whatever. These events were part of life yet seemed like impassable barriers, completely blocking the path and bringing each journey to an end. I know that to succeed I must negotiate a way around these obstacles. I could not afford to fail at the first one. Where would I end up? How much worse would life get? What would it eventually take to make me stop, if not this time?

That evening I was tired and looking forward to a lovely sleep. I stumbled across a couple of thoughts that were to help me a great deal in the face of temptation. I wondered what would be the point of a drink? We were not going to linger over dinner. The evening would be short.

What was the point in having one or two? What was the point anyway?

I decided I would not drink that night but promised myself if I really wanted to drink the following night then I could reconsider it then. I would re-visit my decision each time the opportunity to drink presented itself and ask myself, 'What would be the point?', safe in the knowledge that I could always have it the next time.

After the interminable hour with a diet coke we went to the restaurant at seven o'clock. We were seated and I ordered sparkling water. The restaurant was very busy and the waiters were struggling to keep up. Our drinks took a while to arrive and I thought how agitated and angry I would be if I were awaiting my next glass of wine. I observed a man at the next table rapidly draining his small glass of wine and looking around, desperate to catch the eye of a passing waiter to order another. I felt momentarily glad that tonight, that wasn't me. When he succeeded I watched him press a generous tip into the waiter's palm and indicate that the wine should be kept coming. This method seemed to work and I watched him receive and drink six glasses of wine within an hour. I felt a mixture of envy and annoyance that it was not me. I had self imposed this no alcohol rule and felt truly deprived with my sparkling water. The evening seemed incomplete without wine with dinner. We enjoyed our meal but there was no reason to linger and we left. I looked forward to another evening meal tomorrow where I could, if I wished, drink wine.

I had a great sleep that night and awoke the next morning full of vigour, very glad I had not had six glasses of wine the previous night. It was so obvious that I had made the right choice. Now the morning had come I did not regret not drinking the night before. I vowed to remember these thoughts and feelings when sun-down came again.

During a previous flirtation with sobriety, I had some wise counsel. After hearing of all my failed attempts at all sorts of moderation he suggested simply, just stopping. I would then not need to control it, to monitor it, to ration it or to long for the next time it was allowed. What had I to lose from six months of sobriety? Why not try it, just for a while, give it a fair chance and if I didn't like it, go back to my old habits, was his suggestion. "Those habits will still be there, waiting to welcome you back," he said. At this point in time, I gave this strategy some more thought. Instead of viewing every event where I would usually drink as a barrier to going tee-total, I should accept they would occur and let them. I could experience them without alcohol, just to see, however difficult that may be. So every hurdle I approached I reminded myself I had been to these events many times before and drunk alcohol. I'd had many holidays with wine every night. I'd had many drunken nights out. I knew exactly what they were like and they were always the same. Why not try going without? Why not change the record? Why not try it just this once sober and if it is truly awful, return to drinking alcohol at the next one? I gave reckless me a talking to from sensible me. The type I would give to a friend who I could see making the same mistake over and over again, wondering why it kept happening. I knew if something was going to change, something had to change. I needed to try something radically different, just for a while.

The mental safety net of just this once, just for tonight, just for a time, just for just now, kept me calm. I knew I could always change my mind and drink if I wanted to. One day at a time is a cliche but this open door kept me from becoming overwhelmed to the point of panic by the magnitude of 'forever' and helped me get through those very difficult early days. I had no guarantee of what the next day would bring and I had no pressure to commit to it being alcohol free. All I had to think about was choosing not to drink, just for now.

Chapter 2 Then

The pattern of alcohol use and abuse is that of a gradual and relentless increase in the amount consumed over time. Intake may go up and down but the general trend is always upwards. The use becomes abuse and the choice becomes a need. The time and space required to meet the increasing demands of alcohol grow and grow and begin to overshadow all other aspects of life. There need not be a typical rock bottom calamity nor waiting to become a down-and-out type drinker of value cider at 9am on a Monday morning in the park. The action point is different for everyone and occurs when the realisation dawns that by trying and failing to control alcohol, you actually have no control over it at all. Alcohol is the boss and will continue its take over of your life to the detriment of everything else. It becomes the dominating force. Life as you know it becomes increasingly compromised as alcohol takes hold and invades all areas. So strong is its pull that everything else starts to slide, gradually at first but increasing with time until breaking point is reached. Here, life becomes unmanageable and this is the time to recognise that alcohol can no longer stay in your life.

It took me a long time to reach this conclusion. Longer to accept it and even longer to decide to do something about it. Like many, I tried all sorts of rules and restrictions to moderate my intake of alcohol in increasingly desperate attempts to avoid giving it up completely, an option I could not seriously contemplate. My regulations were usually formulated during a hangover and were to allow some alcohol and avoid the need to go completely alcohol free.

The rules started off very rigid and restrictive in theory, drinking only on one weekend a month for example, but became increasingly lax as reality struck. I would think I had set the bar too high to succeed so would revise my allowance up to every weekend. I may throw in a not-in-the-house or not-when-alone rule too. Over short periods of time, as memories of the last awful hangover faded, I would include Thursday nights in the weekend (as Friday is often my day off). Soon, an unfinished bottle of wine from Sunday would be drunk on Monday night. Before long a mid-week restorative drink was allowed back in and soon I would be drinking most nights of the week again. My intake each time would increase. If I had a bottle of wine on a Thursday it seemed natural to have more on a Friday and Saturday. Eventually this behaviour would culminate in another terrible hangover, during which I would invent another set of rules and scare myself with the deal that if I did not stick to the plan THIS time, I would have to go completely alcohol-free.

Eventually I admitted these strategies failed to help. I was no further forward in my quest to control my alcohol intake. I was sick and tired of failing, and failing by making the same mistakes time after time. I resigned myself sadly to the fact that my only remaining option was to become alcohol free in the long term. The next question was when. When would this seismic lifestyle change occur? The answer was vague and always at some indistinct point in the future. It was certainly not Now.

I reached my Now about 18 months before my third and final attempt to stop drinking. It was my first of two failed but significant attempts and arose in part out of necessity. My drinking patterns were changing, my intake increasing and my life unmanageable. My drinking was restricting my life and was no longer a positive experience. I now 'needed' a certain amount each evening (or so I believed). I was no longer relaxing with the first glass. I began to drink earlier, faster. I was finding more and more opportunities to drink and if there were none, I would make them up. I arranged nights out and dinner parties all of which revolved around drinking, on the pretext of 'catching up'. If I was working one night I had to make sure I could drink the night before and the night after to the detriment of all other evening activities which did not involve or permit alcohol. I began to notice my drinking was different from others. I would note my Other Half (OH) having A glass of wine with dinner and being content, whilst I polished off the bottle and looked for more. I noticed a friend be given a glass of wine and continue to chat for half an hour before she took her first sip. Wine had become the focus in my life and I believed I was only happy at times when I was drinking it. Once while arranging a girls night out, a friend added "And we could all have a little drinkie too!!" almost as an afterthought whereas for me it was the whole point of going out.

My first action point arrived after one particular night out. It was late November. A weekday night. A low key catch up with a friend before the Christmas melee began. I had a gin and tonic or two whilst getting ready, unable to bear the anticipation of waiting any longer. Who knew how many units were in each home poured glass? Then down to my friend's house for a quick one before the taxi arrived.

We arrived pleasantly drunk at the small, quiet bistro, and ordered our first bottle of wine. The chat flowed, the vibes were good, the waiters interactive and before we knew it the bottle was finished. But I had a partner in crime and we ordered a second bottle, thinking it was a good idea, while knowing it was a bad idea but hey, we could deal with that tomorrow. Right now, it was a good idea.

Waiting for it to arrive allowed time for my rapid intake over the last 90 minutes to kick home. I suddenly felt very drunk and was once again annoyed with myself that this had happened. It was a small establishment, relatively quiet. I was conspicuous. I was overly familiar with fellow diners. I made obvious, staggering and frequent, trips to the Ladies, claiming an upset stomach. I could no longer focus or converse. I felt so ill and was using all my willpower not to be sick in public.

The evening was cut short and we left very suddenly. I could not drink any more. I had to get out for fresh air. I left my friend to pay, to order a taxi, and to get me into and out of it. I was incapable of doing any of those things. I was truly paralytic, mute, helpless but remained aware enough to feel embarrassed and ashamed. Why did I always end up over doing it, never knowing when enough was enough? Alcohol had failed to enhance the evening, failed to make me happy and had left me with a huge helping of negative feelings and emotions. Drinking alcohol was no longer fun and I couldn't carry on like this.

Admitting it was now a problem to myself was a significant step, but voicing it to another seemed to confirm the reality of it all. I had once heard a recovering alcoholic speak at a conference. He was 60 years old and had been sober for many years. He explained to the audience the depths to which alcohol had taken his life. The havoc it caused. He spoke of the disabling effects that drinking alcohol wreaked upon normal daily activities. I was stunned by his frankness, his humility and his willingness to share such unpleasant events with the audience. He finished by telling us the details of a support group he had set up to help people like us, if we were ever to find ourselves in a similar situation. Perhaps it was just me but there was a real sense of unease in the room, the message was too close to home for many of us I suspect. Now, I dug out that telephone number and after much deliberation (what would I say? where would I start?), I made the call.

It was a good move but very difficult. It made me face up to the severity of my pattern of drinking and I was quickly in tears. This stranger at the end of the line told the truth, without sentiment or platitudes. He never once reassured me that I wasn't that bad or was no worse than anyone else. He never rubbished my concerns that I may have a problem. He calmly listened and made me acknowledge that simply by taking this huge step of phoning, meant there was indeed a problem. He asked probing questions that friends and family would not dare to. Had I ever driven whilst drunk? Had I drunk alcohol while pregnant? Did I drink in the morning? He was not surprised by any of my answers, calmly accepting them as he had with countless others, many times before I'm sure. This was the first time I had faced the facts head on. I recounted my efforts to moderate and my disappointment that none of them worked. His response was to laugh and say 'Well give up totally then'. It sounded so simple yet I knew it was impossible. And anyway, I didn't want to stop. I wanted to normalise my drinking. Even just the thought of stopping completely filled me with horror and fear. A multitude of upcoming events flashed into my mind. Christmas. New Year. A conference I was going to. What about my Friday night bottle of wine? What would I do? No, I was not ready to stop and I knew I would not be able to do it. But I had to try something. I decided I would see how long I could last without any alcohol. I had previously managed without for a ten day stretch whilst dieting like mad for a holiday (although more commonly switched from wine to spirits and low cal mixers at these times). It wasn't an absolute or intended abstinence.

It was mid December when I first started to stop. I counted the days which made me feel proud and sad at the same time. Proud I had gone a week without alcohol but sad that this was such a remarkable achievement. I found my usual drinking start time the hardest and went to great lengths to keep busy and distracted. Just like anything else, not being able to have it makes you want it even more. About this time a new social networking site, www.soberistas.com, had just been launched. a site for people who are concerned about the role of alcohol in their lives and wish to address or change this in some way. I had no experience of social networking and to date do not frequent any other sites, but this one was to become a huge factor in my eventual success. Instead of drinking I could visit the site to recount my difficulties, moan that it wasn't fair, ask for help and advice, ask what others do, or just vent.

Many emotions seem to wake up and want out when the dulling, damping effect of alcohol is removed. I had a million thoughts and emotions all trying to be heard. Under a cloak of relative anonymity afforded by my username, typing these out-pourings became a huge means of pressure relief. They were no longer all bottled up inside. I found I could 'speak' openly and honestly, perhaps like never before, and have several responses in seconds from non judgmental people in similar positions. I read and read all around the site and gradually began to think that maybe I could do this after all.

So, I drove to my few Christmas parties and had soft drinks when a group of friends came round. Each time I felt excited and vaguely high on the party atmosphere and copious amounts of caffeinated soft drinks. I left parties pleased in the knowledge that I hadn't done anything stupid or embarrassing. I was a better hostess and spoke to all my friends without becoming overbearing. I cleared up when they left without eating all the remaining snacks and nibbles. The mornings after were fantastic. I marvelled at the sheer novelty of having a night out and remaining functional the following day. There was no price to pay. It seemed like a huge reward for the effort afforded and reinforced the notion that alcohol free socialising was possible, perhaps even enjoyable, and was a much better way to live.

I lasted just under three weeks. Nineteen days to be precise. My change of heart came as a bolt from the blue. It is said that people revert to alcohol at times of extreme sadness or immense happiness. For me it was the latter. Between Christmas and New Year I had taken delivery of a new car one morning. I felt so buoyant and happy. We were having good friends round the same afternoon, ones with whom we always have champagne, then wine, then more wine. I had not planned how I was going to break the news that I wouldn't be drinking and I was worried my friends would be disappointed, and feel that I was spoiling the occasion. I was still in a quandary when they arrived. The champagne popped and I suddenly thought 'Yes, I will have some. I want to maximise this buoyant feeling and really enjoy the company of my friends'. I did not want to miss out anything anymore. I had felt like a martyr to the cause at Christmas, trying to prove to myself I did not need booze. And I did not need it, but I thought it would make a good day even better. So the occasion turned out the same way as those times before; champagne and snacks, a nice meal and wine, more wine for the ladies and our friends leaving around eight o'clock. We had all had enough and the event was over. But I couldn't stop. At times like this I would busy myself in the kitchen clearing up, all the while drinking more wine. Once finished I would sit down and 'relax' after all my efforts with yet another well deserved glass of wine, only stopping when I fell asleep.

I tried not to be too hard on myself and my thoughts of the last three weeks changed. I didn't need to be absolutely abstinent. Those people I had chatted with on soberistas.com had got it wrong. They were being overly strict and missing out on good times and even better times by not ever having alcohol. It was unnecessary self deprivation. I stopped logging on to chat or report. That way of life was not for me.

For the rest of the festive holiday period I well and truly let my hair down, making up for lost time.

At the beginning of January I planned to drink alcohol only at special occasions and at some weekends on the rare occasion my OH wanted a glass of wine with dinner. Regular drinking each night would stop and it being Friday would not in itself be deemed a special occasion. For the next year the pattern was wine on Friday and Saturdays. This quickly included Thursdays and Sundays, to round off the weekend. Before long I was convincing myself that a mid week treat on a Wednesday was acceptable and after a Monday I'd need to relax with a glass of wine after 'the first day back'. Very quickly I was back to drinking most evenings. Then the amount I was drinking each night would increase. I once plucked up the courage to ask my OH if he thought I drank too much. He said of course not, it wasn't as if I was downing a bottle of wine a night, was it? Perhaps not, but it wasn't far off.

I took a bottle of wine per night to be the critical amount defining problem drinking and began to restrict myself to 3/4 of a bottle at a time. Or just leaving a little in the bottle. Or finishing it and putting water in the bottle to look as though there was still some left and make a show of pouring it away the next night, preferring a fresh bottle.

More and more to drink would become the norm until again, I revisited the notion of sobriety in my head. I'd toy with it and think it through and always come up with the same answer; that I did not want to stop totally. The deal I made with myself was that if I did not stick to my own rules about when and how much it was permissible to drink, then I would have no option but to become tee-total. My resistance to this option was such that I hoped it would motivate and incentivise me to abide by the restriction and moderation plan.

It didn't.

Time and time again I would bend my rules and end up in the same situation, doing the same things I had sworn I would never do again, and having the same awful feelings, both mentally and physically, the next day. Making the same mistakes over and over again is so demoralising and I was not able to see the futility of doing the same things time after time yet expecting a different outcome. If something's going to change, something has to change.

Not until a full year later did I decide I would change. I would start in January of course. Complete abstinence continued to feel an extreme and unrealistic option doomed to fail so I would be doing the next best thing. Alcohol would be for special occasions only, once per month maximum.

Of course in preparation, I had drunk wine every night over Christmas and New Year. I was left bloated, overly full, fat and tired. I needed a rest, perhaps even a rest from wine I acknowledged. On the 3rd January I identified the 31st January as being the next time I would drink. I would be away overnight due to work, and with colleagues. As always it would be very sociable. I counted the days free from booze and passed my previous nineteen day abstinence record of the year before. Each day was more of a struggle than the one before and it was getting harder instead of easier. My want was building and was becoming increasingly difficult to control. It was as if a pressure was building up inside me with nowhere to go, no means of escape, until one day when it would erupt and I would end up drunk once again. My mindset was entirely of when will this time be up? When can I cave to release and relax? When will this torture be over?

On 26th January after a stressful day of children's birthday parties I felt I absolutely needed a drink and moreover, I deserved one. I hated the fact that it was a need rather than a choice but I was strung out and harassed and it was the only way to cope. Anyway, it was almost the 31st when I had planned to drink anyway so a few days early would not make much difference.

It did.

Apart from having far too much in order to relax that night, a mindset developed whereby I thought there seemed to be no benefit in starting to stop again when I knew it would only be for a couple of days until the next planned day for drinking. I drank every night up to and including the 31st. Afterwards, I had planned not to drink until the end of February, another month away. This was good. It gave me the good run I needed at it, free from obligatory drinking events to make it worthwhile stopping. Sadly I could not recapture the resolve and motivation of January 3rd and I succumbed after only a few days. Frustrated by myself and my continued failure I wondered, what was the point? What to do now?

I pushed the thought momentarily to the back of my mind and continued to drink wine.

For the rest of the month I did pretty much what I liked, drank what I wanted when I wanted it (and even at times when I did not really want it). In March three things happened that finally brought things to a head. Firstly, a night out for a celebratory dinner with a group of colleagues. I became overly drunk and made a complete fool of myself. I felt so stupid the next day and cringe even now to remember it such that I cannot bear to write it down. Secondly we had arranged to have some good friends around for dinner towards the end of the month, just before our two week break. It was a Friday public holiday and I was really looking forward to their company and the free flow of wine we always shared. I felt the holiday really began for me a day early, on Thursday night. When I finished work, I relaxed with some wine at home. I had more and more, much more than I intended. Too much in fact, even though it was the holidays. My hangover the next day was the worst imaginable and completely ruined my usual enjoyment of preparing for guests. I just wanted to curl up on the sofa, cancel them, and have everyone leave me alone.

When they first arrived around mid afternoon I could not yet face a glass of wine. Only after a couple of hours and a few salty snacks did I tentatively start on the wine, cautiously at first before quickly gaining momentum. And again, once started I could not stop. I was not enjoying it. I felt as if I was poisoning myself. This had happened more than once lately and I now bought more and more expensive wine, thinking I would enjoy it better, it being of a higher quality. Truth be told I was past any enjoyment. I was stuck in a drinking loop of self destructive necessity and I was powerless to extricate myself.

Subsequently I suffered a cumulative hangover that had built up over the preceding 48 hour period. I accepted then that I was failing at any form of moderation and that I needed to stop drinking completely. Things had changed from my vowing never to drink again to knowing that I could not and should not, ever drink. This time, failure was not an option. The consequences were too terrifying. Complete abstinence was the only way out of this situation. I'd tried and failed at everything else and was fed up with it. I was fed up opening wine almost against my will thinking, 'Here we go again'. I was fed up being unable to do what I wanted. I was fed up making the same mistakes. How could it be so difficult not to do something? Why not just, not do it?

To compound my misery, anxiety and self-loathing the third thing going on was my imminent holiday. I was worried about how I was going to cope. We were going away to the sun the next day on an all inclusive break. I was worried about the free and freely available alcohol, drinking too much, drinking every day, being able to drink earlier and for longer. Being freed from driving and many of my home responsibilities and their inherent restrictive effect meant I had no means to control my intake and no strategy to cope. Left to chance, it would dominate my holiday and ruin it. I knew I had to stop drinking completely but now was not the time to do it. I had not yet thought about when that right time may be, but for sure, it was not right now.

I logged back into soberistas.com to canvas opinion about what to do on my holiday. It is said that advice is something you ask for when you know the correct answer, but wish you didn't. I wasn't brave enough to decide to stop drinking right before this holiday; holidays and alcohol go hand in hand after all. I think I needed to hear it from someone else, to hear some objectivity. As ever I received several replies within minutes. All of them rational. None of them judgmental. Some suggested ways to moderate; drink on alternate days of the holiday, don't drink before 6pm or after 10pm. Some suggested drinking very mindfully and thinking about exactly what I was getting from it, then plan to give up on returning home. One memorable reply came straight to the point. Stop now. Just stop now. Is it really going to be any easier to stop in two weeks time when combined with the post-holiday gloom and the return of daily stressors in the working week? No. Why spoil the holiday by drinking more than ever? Take the time away as an opportunity for nurturing and pampering yourself. Avoid the toxins of alcohol and come home refreshed and glowing, having conquered the first two weeks of an alcohol-free life.

This seemed a complete anathema to me, at odds with my default thoughts of 'it's 'free' so have as much as possible, I'm on holiday so I deserve it and I'm on holiday so I will have even more,' yet at some level I knew it was right. The seed had been planted and the notion grew and grew, filling my head with all the additional ramifications. Knowing it was right did not make it any easier. Quite the opposite. It increased my sense of panic as I knew that was what I had to do. Failing again was not an option. After my false starts, I had to do it this time. I couldn't bear to imagine the alternative. I have had many holidays drinking wine each night. The patterns are always the same and now I wanted to stop but felt unsure if I could do it. I decided I would try one holiday without booze. It was unfortunate that it coincided with this all inclusive trip but there would be others and if it was truly dull and boring I could always revert back to drinking at the next holiday. What did I have to lose?

****

The rest of Sober is the New Black is available on Amazon.

And finally if you are a life long dieter or swapped the wine witch for chocolate, cake and other crap carbs, then have a look at <u>Sweet and Sober</u> and realise you are not alone.

If you enjoy these books perhaps you would consider writing a short review on Amazon for the benefit of others. Please also feel free to share on your social media if you want to help spread the sober is better message, and as always keep in touch via my blog

www.soberisthenewrachelblack.blogspot.co.uk

or follow me on Twitter @SoberRachel

It's always lovely to hear from you.

Best wishes

Rachel x

Printed in Great Britain
by Amazon.co.uk, Ltd.,
Marston Gate.